First U.S. edition 2020
First published by Big Picture Press, an imprint of Bonnier Books U.K. 2020

Library of Congress Catalog Card Number pending
ISBN 978-1-5362-0310-3

20 21 22 23 24 25 LEO 10 9 8 7 6 5 4 3 2 1

Printed in Heshan, Guangdong, China

This book was typeset in PiS Creatinin Pro.
The illustrations were created digitally.

BIG PICTURE PRESS
an imprint of
Candlewick Press
99 Dover Street
Somerville, Massachusetts 02144

www.candlewick.com

CITIES IN LAYERS

Six Famous Cities through Time

PHILIP STEELE

ILLUSTRATED BY
ANDRÉS LOZANO

BPP

CITIES IN LAYERS

Humans have been building cities for thousands of years. In this book you can explore major metropolises now and at different times in the past.

12

ROME, ITALY

TODAY • 1580 • 203 CE

In the former capital of the Roman Empire, we can still walk the same streets as emperors.

20

ISTANBUL, TURKEY

TODAY • 1616 • 550 CE

Known by the ancient Romans as Constantinople, Istanbul is the only city that spans two continents.

28

PARIS, FRANCE

TODAY • 1793 • 1380

Home of the Eiffel Tower, this city is famous for its revolutions, universities, and artists.

Find the red flag in each city to begin your tour!

36

BEIJING, CHINA

TODAY • 1912 • 1553

The glittering modern metropolis overlies an ancient city of palaces, temples, lakes, and gardens.

44

LONDON, U.K.

TODAY • 1863 • 1613

London is a buzzing economic center where traces of Roman and medieval cities can be found.

52

NEW YORK CITY, U.S.A.

TODAY • 1931 • 1886

The famous skyscrapers of Manhattan's towering skyline are symbols of the modern world.

WHAT IS A CITY?

A city is a large settlement of people, which may have special importance as a center of government, religion, or trade. Humans have been building cities for thousands of years. In this book you will visit six cities at different periods in their history. These cities have all changed and grown over time as populations have increased, power has changed hands, and technology has developed.

HOW CITIES BEGAN

The earliest cities were built in prehistoric times, when people were learning how to farm crops and raise livestock. Farming meant that humans no longer had to be nomadic hunters to survive and that they could settle in one place and store food. This new way of life allowed more time to work at crafts, to find out about the world, and to develop writing and counting.

WALLS AND DEFENSES

There is safety in numbers, and cities offer security to the people who live there. The first cities were surrounded by thick walls for defense against attacking armies. The most famous defensive walls of the ancient world surrounded Rome and Constantinople (today's Istanbul).

All the cities in this book had city walls in the past, except for New York — by the time it was built, powerful guns been invented that made city walls obsolete. But even New York began as a military fortification, called Fort Amsterdam, in the 17th century.

WATER AND DRAINS

No city can survive without a supply of fresh water for people to drink. Many cities were built beside rivers such as the river Seine in Paris or the river Thames in London. Both Rome and Constantinople brought spring water into the city from the countryside, along water channels called aqueducts.

Rivers are also used for drainage. One of the earliest sewers was Rome's Cloaca Maxima, which carried waste into the river Tiber. By the industrial age of the 1800s, factory waste and sewage from London were polluting the water of the Thames, spreading deadly diseases.

MONUMENTS

Every city has its famous landmarks. Many have become symbols of the city, which are instantly recognized around the world — such as the Statue of Liberty in New York or the Eiffel Tower in Paris. Monuments may be grand tombs, statues, triumphal arches, war memorials, tall columns, or beautiful fountains. They may be built to honor gods or kings and queens, to commemorate important events or battles, to impress visitors, or just to make the city look beautiful. Some stone columns called obelisks were taken from ancient Egyptian cities such as Thebes to adorn later capitals, such as Rome, Paris, and London. Monuments don't just help us find our way around cities — they tell us stories of the distant and more recent past.

ROADS AND RAILS

For thousands of years the main form of transport was by horse, boat, or foot. Many ancient cities were shaped by their roads, which allowed soldiers and merchants to move through and between cities quickly. The coming of railways in the 19th century transformed all the cities in this book. In the 20th century, the popularity of cars also changed many cities. Today multilane motorways like Beijing's distinctive ring roads are humming hubs of transport.

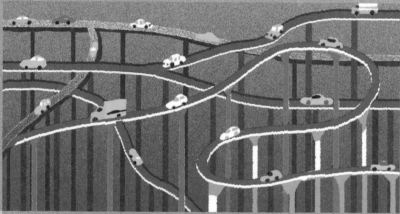

BRIDGES AND BOATS

Rivers and canals were used by ships and barges for carrying goods. An ancient Grand Canal linked northern China with rice-growing regions to the south and eventually served Beijing. In cities such as London in the 1500s, small boats were used to ferry passengers around, like the taxis of today. For cities to grow, they needed bridges so that people and carts could get across waterways more quickly. Many bridges became famous landmarks.

BUILDINGS

The first cities were built from locally available materials like clay, timber, and straw. More durable stone was often used for city walls, temples, or royal palaces. Ordinary people lived in crowded and poorly built homes where fires were common. Rome was devastated by fire in 64 CE and London in 1666.

Often the finest buildings were reserved for gods. Medieval Christian cathedrals soared into the sky. In the 1500s the skyline of Muslim Istanbul became filled with the domes and minarets (prayer towers) of great mosques. But even these spires have been eclipsed in the modern age of skyscrapers.

SIX CITIES THROUGH TIME

ROME

753 BCE
The legendary founding of Rome.

27 BCE
Augustus becomes the first emperor of Rome.

70–80 CE
The huge amphitheater, the Colosseum, is built.

380 CE
Christianity becomes Rome's official religion.

AD 476
Rome's power declines as its last emperor is deposed.

ISTANBUL

657 BCE
Greek traders found a colony called Byzantium.

196 CE
Emperor Septimius Severus captures the city and expands it.

324 CE
Emperor Constantine rebuilds the city and names it Constantinople.

537 CE
The church of Hagia Sophia is completed.

1204
Christian knights loot the city during the Fourth Crusade.

PARIS

52 BCE
The Romans defeat the Gaulish tribes and build a town called Lutetia.

486 CE
Paris is ruled by Clovis I, king of the Franks.

845 CE
Repeated Viking attacks culminate in the Siege of Paris.

1163–1345
The building of Notre-Dame Cathedral.

BEIJING

1045–221 BCE
The rise of Jicheng, the first city built on this site.

1215–1293
Mongols destroy the city. It is rebuilt as Dadu, the capital of the Yuan dynasty.

1368
The Ming dynasty is founded — they rule China for 276 years.

LONDON

43 CE
Romans found the settlement of Londinium.

490 CE
Saxons control the London area. Their settlement is called Lundenwic.

1066
The Norman Conquest begins.

NEW YORK CITY

1508
Michelangelo starts painting the ceiling of the Sistine Chapel.

1870
Rome becomes the capital city of a new, united nation of Italy.

1957
The Treaty of Rome sets in motion the process that will later form the European Union.

1453
The city falls to an army of Muslim Turks. It becomes the capital of the Ottoman Empire and is informally called Istanbul.

1918–1923
The fall of the Ottoman Empire. In 1923 the new Republic of Turkey moves the capital to Ankara.

1682
King Louis XIV moves to the Palace of Versailles.

1789–1799
The French Revolution overthrows the monarchy.

1804
Napoleon I is crowned emperor.

1887–1889
The Eiffel Tower is constructed.

1406–1420
The imperial palace complex is built. It is known as the "Forbidden City."

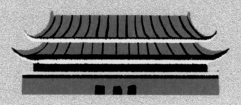

1899
The start of the Boxer Rebellion — a revolt against foreign influence in China.

1912
The end of imperial rule in China. Sun Yat-sen declares China a republic.

1949
Mao Zedong forms the People's Republic of China.

2010
China becomes the world's second largest economy.

1599
Shakespeare's Globe Theatre is built in Southwark.

1642–1651
Civil War breaks out and King Charles I is executed.

1665–1666
The Great Plague is followed by the Great Fire of London.

1837–1901
Queen Victoria rules the British Empire. London is the world's largest city.

2012
The Shard (1,004 ft./ 306 m) becomes the tallest building in the United Kingdom.

1524
The Lenape people live on the island of Manna-hata.

1626
The Dutch begin to forcibly remove the Lenape people from the island of Manna-hata, which is later renamed Manhattan.

1674
England gains possession of New York through the Treaty of Westminster.

1775
The American Revolution begins.

1886
The Statue of Liberty is unveiled.

1929
The Wall Street Crash starts a global financial crisis.

2012
New York's tallest building is One World Trade Center.

ROME

The sun is rising over the rooftops of Rome, as it has done for centuries.
It lights up the dome of St. Peter's Basilica and sparkles on the river Tiber.

ROME

Country: Italy

Continent: Europe

Estimated population: 4.2 million
(Greater Rome, 2018)

Founded in: 753 BCE, according to
Roman tradition

Historic name: Roma

WHO HAS LIVED THERE?

Pope Francis (1936–) was born in Argentina. He is the 266th pope, which is the title given to the head of the Roman Catholic Church. Visitors to Rome may see him at midday on Sundays when he gives a papal blessing in St. Peter's Square. When a new pope is elected, thousands of pilgrims gather in the square to await the result.

Michelangelo Buonarroti (1475–1564) was one of the most famous painters and sculptors of Italy's High Renaissance. He painted the ceiling of the famous Sistine Chapel and worked as an architect on St. Peter's Basilica. Michelangelo died in 1564, but his work can still be seen all over Rome.

Septimius Severus (145–211 CE) was born in the ancient city of Leptis Magna in Roman North Africa and was a successful general. In 193 CE his troops proclaimed him emperor after a period of political strife caused by the brutal rule of the emperor Commodus. Septimius Severus died in the town of Eboracum (modern York), in Britain.

ROME TODAY

Rome has been the capital of Italy since 1871, after unification of the country in 1861. At Rome's heart is Vatican City, the world's smallest nation and headquarters of the Catholic Church. The river Tiber flows through Rome on its journey from the Apennine Mountains to the sea.

Noisy traffic flows through the streets of Rome too, as do crowds of people. Rome has high-tech industries and exciting new architecture, fashionable shops and cafés, sporting arenas, and film studios, including Luce Cinecittá.

Many visitors, however, come here to travel back in time. They want to see the city that shaped world history as the mighty capital of the ancient Roman Empire. The impressive ruins of ancient Rome can be found throughout the city.

ROME 1580

Rome in 1580 had fine city squares, and churches filled with glorious paintings. Palaces were built for wealthy bankers and for the pope, who at this time ruled Rome and parts of Italy. From 1506 to 1626 a new basilica of St. Peter's was built — the world's biggest church at the time.

Italy, and much of Europe, was going through huge social changes. From the 1400s to the 1600s, there was a growing thirst for knowledge about the classical world. This inspired exciting new ideas about art and science. We call this period the Renaissance, meaning "rebirth." The famous artists Leonardo da Vinci (1452–1519) and Michelangelo (1475–1564) worked during this era.

In the Middle Ages, Rome had been a city in decline. At one point its population was just 30,000. Medieval Rome was a center of Christianity, but it was still a small city compared with when it had been the heart of the Roman Empire.

The first basilica of St. Peter was completed in 333 CE, after Christianity became legal. In 476 CE, Germanic invaders sacked Rome and overthrew the Roman Empire in the west. Much ancient knowledge was lost in the years that followed.

ROME 203 CE

In 203 CE, Rome was the largest city on Earth, home to a million people and the heart of the Roman Empire. At its height the empire covered around 2 million square mi./5 million square km in Europe, Asia, and Africa. All roads led to Rome.

In the city, temples honored ancient gods, and palaces topped the Palatine Hill, which overlooked the Forum. There Romans met to do business and gossip about gladiators fighting in the Colosseum. Rome's emperor at this time was Septimius Severus. Emperors ruled Rome from 27 BCE to 476 CE.

Even as far back as 203 CE, Rome was already an ancient city. From 509 BCE it had been a republic ruled by elected magistrates and a senate, and it controlled all of Italy by 250 BCE. Romans might have told you that their city was founded in 753 BCE, that their first king was Romulus, and that as a baby he had been raised by a she-wolf. The tale was a myth, but what about that date? Archaeologists now believe that the area was settled even earlier, sometime before 1300 BCE.

FIND THE RED FLAG TO BEGIN YOUR TOUR OF THIS CITY IN LAYERS.

ROME TODAY

Over 2,000 years ago, writers were
calling Rome the "eternal city."
It is still full of life today.

❶ CASTEL SANT'ANGELO
Now a museum, this was once a grim fortress, and
before that an emperor's tomb.

❷ VATICAN CITY
Within the city of Rome is the world's smallest
independent state, Vatican City. The Vatican Palace was
made the pope's official home in 1589. Today visitors
come to admire the Vatican's collection of art — some of
it ancient — and the famous Sistine Chapel.

❸ ST. PETER'S BASILICA
Catholic pilgrims come to see this great church,
completed in 1626. They gather for services in

St. Peter's Square, in which stands one of Rome's 13
ancient Egyptian obelisks.

❹ OLYMPIC STADIUM
Rome's biggest sports stadium hosts AS Roma and
SS Lazio soccer clubs.

❺ TRASTEVERE
Students and buskers fill the narrow streets and
squares around the Basilica of Santa Maria in the
district of Trastevere.

❻ MAXXI
This museum, opened in 2010, displays cutting-edge
21st-century art.

❼ PARCO DELLA MUSICA
Three fine concert halls and an open-air theater
opened here in 2002.

❽ PIAZZA DEL POPOLO
Another ancient Egyptian obelisk towers over this
oval-shaped piazza (town square). This one once

stood in the Circus Maximus of ancient Rome.

❾ TERMINI RAILWAY STATION
Termini has been Rome's biggest and busiest station
since 1862.

❿ AURELIAN WALLS
Today you can still see the remains of the walls that
defended the city of Rome from 275 CE until 1870.

⓫ SPANISH STEPS
These 138 stone steps from the Piazza di Spagna
were completed in 1725.

⓬ PANTHEON
This Roman temple is now a church. Millions of
visitors come every year to marvel at its huge dome.

⓭ TREVI FOUNTAIN
This fantastic fountain dates from 1762. In 19 BCE it
was the end of the Aqua Virgo aqueduct.

⓮ PIAZZA NAVONA
The square, built on the site of the Stadium of

Domitian in 86 CE, is still in the shape of the ancient racetrack. Today it is full of performers and tourists.

15 THEATER OF MARCELLUS
The remains of an ancient Roman open-air theater, dating from 12 BCE, still stand near the Tiber.

16 CIRCUS MAXIMUS PARK
A public park now covers the remains of ancient Rome's chief racetrack.

17 PALATINE HILL
Archaeologists have found evidence of human settlement on the Palatine Hill dating from the 10th century BCE. It was believed that Romulus and Remus, the legendary founders of Rome, were fed by a she-wolf on its slopes. Today visitors may see the ruins of ancient palaces here.

18 COLOSSEUM
This amphitheater, opened in 80 CE, is partly ruined, but still attracts big crowds who shudder to recall the

gladiators who fought to the death there.

19 FORUM
This was Rome's city center from the beginning. It is still occupied by the ruins of many dazzling temples and public buildings.

20 INSULA
In the 20th century, the ruins of a Roman insula (block of apartments) was found near Piazza del Campidoglio.

21 PIAZZA DEL CAMPIDOGLIO
Ancient Rome's Capitoline Hill is topped with Renaissance palaces, which are now museums and the city hall. The equestrian statue in the square shows the emperor Marcus Aurelius. The famous Capitoline Wolf sculpture has been housed in one of the palaces. This depicts Romulus and his brother, Remus, being nursed by the she-wolf, part of the legend of the founding of Rome.

22 IL VITTORIANO
This 1911 monument looks like a giant wedding cake. It was built in honor of the first king of a united Italy, Victor Emmanuel II. Italy became a unified kingdom in 1861. In 1946 it became a republic and the monarchy was abolished.

23 24 25 CHURCHES OF ROME
There are more than 900 churches in Rome. **23** The Jubilee Church has concrete sails like a ship and was built to celebrate the millennium. **24** Basilica of St. John Lateran, built in 314–1735 CE, is an "arch-basilica," the most important of all Roman Catholic churches. **25** Santa Maria Maggiore, built in 432–1750 CE, has played a major part in papal history. Like many churches in Rome, the building tells the story of hundreds of years. The oldest parts of the church date from the 5th century, while the most recent include the 18th-century facade (front).

ROME 1580

By 1580, a Rome of churches and palaces had arisen from the ruins.

① CASTEL SANT'ANGELO
From the 5th century CE, Emperor Hadrian's tomb served as a fortress. The castle's name dates from 590, when the pope saw a vision of the archangel Michael.

② VATICAN CITY
The palaces of the pope, the head of the Catholic Church, are known as the Vatican. The ceiling of the Sistine Chapel was painted by Michelangelo in 1508. It depicts scenes from the Old Testament of the Bible. Michelangelo painted on scaffolding 60 feet above the ground, his neck bent backward as he painted.

The ceiling took four and a half years to complete.

③ ST. PETER'S BASILICA
The first great church on this site was finished in 360 CE, but by the 1400s it was in poor condition. By 1580 the new St. Peter's was rising in its place.

④ TRASTEVERE
Once the center of Rome's Jewish community, this district had small houses and narrow streets.

⑤ SAN PIETRO IN MONTORIO
This medieval church has in its courtyard a perfect little temple, the Tempietto, built in 1502 by the architect Donato Bramante.

⑥ VILLA FARNESINA
This luxury home was built in the 1500s for a rich banker called Agostino Chigi. It was decorated with beautiful wall paintings by the artist Raffaello Sanzio da Urbino, known as Raphael (1483–1520), one of the greatest painters of the Renaissance.

⑦ PONTE SANT'ANGELO
Known in ancient Rome as the Pons Aelius, this bridge across the Tiber was built in 134 CE.

⑧ VILLA MEDICI
The Medici of Florence were one of Renaissance Europe's most rich and powerful families. This grand villa was purchased by them in 1576.

⑨ AURELIAN WALLS
These 3rd-century walls and gatehouses still surrounded Rome in 1580.

⑩ PANTHEON
Famous Renaissance figures, including Raphael, were buried in this ancient Roman temple, which became a Christian church in 609 CE.

⑪ COLUMN OF MARCUS AURELIUS
Climbing the stairs of this ancient column was once a popular pastime.

PIAZZA NAVONA
A busy market moved to this square in the Renaissance times.

PASQUINO
In the 16th century, an ancient statue began to "talk" as citizens posted political messages on it. This tradition continues to this day.

THEATER OF MARCELLUS
This ancient Roman theater became a fortress in the Middle Ages and a palace in 1519.

CIRCUS MAXIMUS
The ancient racecourse fell into disuse and became buried in boggy ground.

COLOSSEUM
The Colosseum had been badly damaged by an earthquake in 1349. Throughout the Renaissance many of its stones were removed from the site to be used on new buildings — including on the rebuilt St. Peter's Basilica. Many fragments of ancient Rome can be found in St. Peter's, including stones in its mosaics.

PALATINE HILL
New buildings were raised among the ancient ruins. One of Europe's first botanical centers, the Farnese Gardens, was planted here in 1550.

FORUM
This important part of the ancient city was abandoned, and cows grazed among the impressive ruins, leading it to be called the Campo Vaccino (cow field).

PIAZZA DEL CAMPIDOGLIO
By the Middle Ages, ancient Rome's sacred Capitoline Hill had become derelict. Michelangelo planned a new square but died in 1564, before it was completed.

BATHS OF DIOCLETIAN
Built between 298 and 306 CE, these were the largest imperial baths. In the 1560s, Michelangelo designed the basilica that was built on some of the remains.

TOWER OF THE MILITIAS
In medieval Italian cities, powerful families built fortified towers like this 12th-century construction.

TRAJAN'S MARKET
Extra floors were added to the remains in the Middle Ages, and a convent was built over part of it in 1574.

CHURCHES OF ROME
Many Catholic pilgrims came to Rome in the Renaissance and continue to visit today. There is a traditional pilgrimage of seven famous churches in Rome, which includes 3 St. Peter's Basilica, under which the tomb of St. Peter is believed to lie; 23 St. Paul Outside the Walls; 24 St. Sebastian Outside the Walls; 25 Basilica of St. John Lateran; 26 Holy Cross in Jerusalem; 27 St. Lawrence Outside the Walls; and 28 Santa Maria Maggiore.

ROME 203 CE

All roads lead to Rome,
the biggest city on Earth . . .

❶ HADRIAN'S MAUSOLEUM
This vast tomb for Emperor Hadrian was built in 135 CE. His wife, Sabina, and other members of his family were also buried there.

❷ NECROPOLIS
Ancient tombs lined the roads approaching Rome, with urns holding ashes of the dead.

❸ CIRCUS OF NERO
This racecourse was built in 40 CE. At its center was an Egyptian obelisk, which today stands in St. Peter's Square. This circus was where the first Christians were executed by the emperor Nero from 65 CE onward. St. Peter was one of these.

❹ RIVER TIBER
Rome lies about 20 mi./30 km inland from the mouth of the river, which was used for transporting goods to the city. Because the city could be reached by river from the Mediterranean Sea, Rome was connected to major trade routes without being on the coast and vulnerable to naval attack.

❺ ROMAN ROADS
The Romans are famous for their long, straight roads. The most famous is the Appian Way, begun in 312 BCE, which linked Rome with southern Italy.

❻ PANTHEON
The Pantheon was a temple that honored all the Roman gods. It was built by Hadrian in 126 CE. Its massive concrete dome weighs 5,000 tons/4,535 metric tons.

❼ COLUMN OF MARCUS AURELIUS
This monument was built around 180 CE to mark the victories of Emperor Marcus Aurelius.

❽ STADIUM OF DOMITIAN
This athletics stadium was a gift to the public from Emperor Domitian, and it opened its gates in 86 CE.

❾ ROMAN BATHS
Rome had many public baths, where men and women gathered to clean themselves, exercise, and socialize.

❿ CLOACA MAXIMA
This sewer has drained the city of Rome of its waste water throughout its history. The Romans even had a goddess of sewers, named Cloacina!

⓫ THEATER OF MARCELLUS
Roman plays followed the Greek tradition, and comedies about Roman life were very popular. This big theater opened in 13 BCE.

⓬ CIRCUS MAXIMUS
The biggest stadium in Rome, this circus held crowds of up to 250,000. It staged races, games, and shows.

13 COLOSSUS OF NERO

A giant statue of the god Sol was moved outside the amphitheater from the palace of the Emperor Nero. Some say it originally represented Nero himself.

14 FLAVIAN AMPHITHEATER

Later nicknamed the "Colosseum" after the enormous statue of Emperor Nero beside it, this building could hold up to 50,000 spectators. They could watch brutal shows, where warriors known as gladiators fought to the death. There were even mock sea battles, when the amphitheater would be flooded with enough water for ships to sail in.

15 FORUM

Rome's original busy downtown area was a center of commerce, politics, law, and religion. Many of Rome's most impressive temples were built here, and it was used for ceremonies, including triumphal processions.

16 17 TRIUMPHAL ARCHES

These were erected in and around the Forum to honor military victories. **16** The Arch of Titus was raised in 81 CE in honor of Emperor Titus, who had besieged Jerusalem. **17** The Arch of Emperor Septimius Severus was the latest addition to the Forum in 203 CE.

18 PALATINE HILL

The power center of ancient Rome, this cluster of palaces had been home to many different emperors.

19 CAPITOLINE HILL

This hill was the city's first stronghold and a holy site. On its top was the temple of the Roman god Jupiter Optimus Maximus ("the greatest and the best"). This was rebuilt four times in its history.

20 TRAJAN'S COLUMN

This spectacular monument was finished around 113 BCE. It was built to commemorate Trajan's victory against a people called the Dacians, who lived in an area that contained parts of modern Romania and Moldova. Its stone carvings tell historians details about the Roman legions and the way they fought.

21 TRAJAN'S MARKET

Perhaps the world's first shopping mall, this busy marketplace center also included luxury apartments.

22 ROMAN INSULAE

Rome was full of three- or four-story blocks of apartments called insulae where poorer citizens lived. They had shops at street level and apartments above. Insulae were crowded and fires often broke out.

23 AQUEDUCTS

In 203 CE, the fountains and public baths of Rome were served by ten aqueducts, which channeled water from the Aniene River and streams in the Apennine Mountains. An eleventh would be added in 226 CE. Aqueducts still stand in parts of the ancient empire, including Istanbul (see pages 20–27).

ISTANBUL

This ancient city lies between two continents, Europe and Asia, and has been a center of trade between them for nearly 2,700 years.

ISTANBUL

Country: Turkey
Continents: Europe and Asia
Estimated population: 14.9 million (2019)
Founded in: 667 BCE (according to tradition)
Historic names: Lygos, Byzantion, Byzantium, New Rome, Constantinople

WHO HAS LIVED THERE?

Sabiha Gökçen (1913–2001) was the adopted daughter of the founder of modern Turkey, Mustafa Kemal Atatürk. In her twenties, Sabiha became fascinated by flying and became a pioneer aviator. Later she became the world's first female combat pilot. Istanbul's Sabiha Gökçen International Airport (2009) is named after her.

Mimar Sinan (c. 1490–1588) was a brilliant architect whose work was unequaled in the Ottoman period. He was born in Ağırnas, a village in modern Turkey's Keyseri Province. Taken to Istanbul for military training, he became famous as an engineer and builder. He designed mosques, schools, palaces, bridges, aqueducts, and baths.

Justinian I and Theodora (Justinian c. 482–565 CE; Theodora c. 500–548 CE) were the rulers of 6th-century Constantinople, a wealthy, powerful city. As emperor, Justinian won back large areas of the old Roman Empire and rewrote Roman law. Justinian's wife, Theodora, was an actress of humble origins who became a powerful empress.

ISTANBUL TODAY

A long strip of blue water stretches from the Black Sea to the Sea of Marmara. It is called the Bosporus, and it separates Europe and Asia. On either side of the Bosporus is Istanbul — the only city in the world built across two continents. A third of Istanbul's population lives on the Asian side of the city.

Although Istanbul is the largest city in the Republic of Turkey, Ankara has been the capital since 1923, when the Republic was founded — four years after the Ottoman Empire was defeated in WWI. Before this, the Ottoman Empire had ruled Turkey for 600 years. At its height, it extended to the Middle East, North Africa, Greece, and Hungary.

To the north of an estuary called the Golden Horn are shopping malls and skyscrapers. The oldest and more residential part of the city lies south of the Golden Horn, where the domes and minarets (towers from which Muslims are called to prayer) of mosques populate the skyline. The famous Hagia Sophia church is now a museum.

ISTANBUL 1616

In 1616, a great new mosque was completed in Istanbul and named after the sultan, Ahmet I, who was a member of the Ottoman, or Osmanli, dynasty. The Osmanli ruled the Ottoman Empire from 1299 to 1923. Istanbul was a Muslim city, but it was also home to Jews and Christians. At this time, the church of Hagia Sophia was a mosque, flanked by four minarets.

The city's water supply was a marvel of engineering and made use of ancient underground reservoirs called cisterns.

The Grand Bazaar was a maze of shops, workshops, warehouses, and merchants' inns. The air smelled of finely ground coffee, which was introduced in the 16th century.

The Ottoman Empire had ruled Istanbul since 1453, when they had used cannons to break through the strong city wall.

Before the Ottomans took the city, it was known as Constantinople and for hundreds of years it had been the center of the Christian Byzantine Empire. It had been in decline since Christian Crusaders sacked it in 1204.

CONSTANTINOPLE 550 CE

In 550 CE, the Byzantine Empire was at the height of its powers and Constantinople was a wealthy city, formidably defended by its famous walls. The empire took its name from Byzantium, the ancient Greek city that once occupied this site. The emperor Justinian I ruled much of the old Roman Empire's lands around the Mediterranean Sea. Constantinople was founded on Roman laws and customs, but it became a city where Greek and many other languages were spoken.

The great domed church of Hagia Sophia towered over a busy marketplace, the Augustaion. The city's main shopping street was called the Mese, and the Hippodrome racetrack lay to the west of the Great Palace.

Emperor Constantine rebuilt the city as a new eastern capital of the Roman Empire in the 4th century. He named it Constantinople after himself, but it was also called New Rome.

Before that it was a Greek colony called Byzantion, said to have been founded in 685–667 BCE, and even earlier the site was a Thracian trading post called Lygos.

ISTANBUL TODAY

Where East meets West.

❶ HAGIA EIRENE
This Byzantine church became the first museum of the Ottoman Empire in 1875. Today it is a concert hall.

❷ TOPKAPI PALACE
This former palace of the Ottoman sultans is now a museum housing a wonderful collection of treasures.

❸ HAGIA SOPHIA MUSEUM
Built in 537 CE, Hagia Sophia was the Church of the Holy Wisdom for 916 years and a mosque for 482. It has been a museum since 1935.

❹ SULTAN AHMET I MOSQUE
Also known as the Blue Mosque, this imposing building is one of the city's most famous landmarks.

❺ BATHS OF ROXELANA (1556)
❻ CAĞALOĞLU BATHS (1741)
Traditional Turkish baths (hamam) are places for socializing, relaxing, and cleansing.

❼ RUINS OF BOUKOLEON
Some of this ancient palace was demolished when the railway line was built along the coast in 1873.

❽ HIPPODROME
Surviving monuments on the site of this ancient racecourse include the Greek Serpent Column and an Egyptian obelisk from 1490 BCE.

❾ LITTLE HAGIA SOPHIA MOSQUE
Completed in 536 CE as a church, this mosque has columns of red and green marble.

❿ TURKISH AND ISLAMIC ARTS MUSEUM
Beautiful tiles and rugs are displayed in this former 16th-century palace.

⓫ COLUMN OF CONSTANTINE
The "burnt pillar" is the remaining section of a Roman column that marked the rebuilding of Byzantium as "New Rome" by the emperor Constantine in 330 CE.

⓬ SIRCEKI STATION
Built in 1890, this was the terminal of the famous rail service the Orient Express. Its passengers included royalty, film stars, and even secret agents.

⓭ NEW MOSQUE (YENI CAMII)
The 1663 Yeni Camii is a famous city landmark.

⓮ GRAND BAZAAR
Built in 1461, the Grand Bazaar is still a key shopping destination in Istanbul. Today it has more than 3,600 shops and is larger than five football fields at 36,700 square yards/30,700 square m.

⓯ SÜLEYMANIYE MOSQUE
Towering over the Golden Horn, this beautiful mosque was built by the great Mimar Sinan in 1550–1557.

16 ISTANBUL UNIVERSITY
A monumental gate leads to Istanbul University, built on the site of the Ottoman Old Palace.

17 BEYAZIT SQUARE
A few remains of the ancient Forum of Theodosius stand near this square and the Beyazıt II Mosque.

18 VALENS AQUEDUCT
The remaining section of the aqueduct that once channeled water into the ancient city spans the Atatürk Boulevard.

19 KARAGÜMRÜK (VEFA) STADIUM
This stadium stands on the site of a former Roman cistern. There are similar sites in the city (**20** and **21**).

22 THEODOSIAN WALLS
Many sections of the 5th-century defensive walls survive today. They were not breached for 800 years.

23 YENIKAPI FERRY TERMINAL
Ferries depart from this transport hub. In 2005, the

Harbor of Theodosius was discovered nearby and more than 35 ancient ships were excavated.

24 BOSPORUS
Ships travel from the Black Sea to the Mediterranean via the Bosporus Strait.

25 GOLDEN HORN
This stretch of water was once a famous harbor.

26 ISTANBUL MODERN
Opened in a former warehouse in 2004, Istanbul Modern is the city's first museum of modern art.

27 DOLMABAHÇE PALACE
This was the administrative center of the Ottoman Empire from late 19th to early 20th centuries.

28 ARAB MOSQUE
Once a Roman Catholic church, this mosque has both medieval gothic and Ottoman architecture.

29 TAKSIM SQUARE
This square at the center of 21st-century Istanbul is

the location of the Independence Monument.

30 GALATA TOWER
In the 1630s this 220 ft./67 m tower was used for a hang-gliding attempt!

31 PERA PALACE HOTEL
Mata Hari, Greta Garbo, and Agatha Christie all used this hotel, which was built in the 1890s.

32 LEVENT AND 33 MASLAK
These two business districts have high-rise skylines.

34 VODAFONE PARK STADIUM
This is the home stadium of the Besiktas JK soccer club.

35 SOUTH OF THE GOLDEN HORN
This is a residential area of the city, linked by ferry, a rail tunnel, and bridges.

ISTANBUL 1616

Sultans built grand mosques and palaces
in the city they ruled from.

❶ HAGIA EIRENE
The Church of Holy Peace was now used as a
gunpowder store for elite guards, or "Janissaries."
❷ NEW PALACE
The center of the Ottoman Empire's power in 1616
was the grand New Palace complex, later known as
Topkapı ("Cannon Gate"). It was built in 1460–1478 by
Sultan Mehmed II, "the Conqueror."
❸ COLUMN OF THE GOTHS
Some of the oldest Roman and Byzantine
monuments, including this granite column, were still
standing in Ottoman times.

❹ HAGIA SOPHIA
The Ottomans had converted the Church of the Holy
Wisdom into a mosque and added tall minarets.
❺ BATHS OF ROXELANA
The Baths of Roxelana were built by the famous
architect Mimar Sinan in 1556. Roxelana, wife of
Suleyman the Magnificent, wielded considerable
political influence and commissioned a number of
public buildings, such as this one.
❻ SULTAN AHMET MOSQUE
In 1616, a new imperial mosque was built on the site
of the Great Palace of Constantinople, which had
fallen into ruin long before the Ottoman conquest.
The mosque was decorated inside with thousands of
blue tiles and became known as the Blue Mosque.
❼ RUINS OF BOUKOLEON
This famous Byzantine palace was already in ruins
before the Ottoman conquest.

❽ LITTLE HAGIA SOPHIA MOSQUE
The former church of Saints Sergius and Bacchus
was converted to a mosque around 1513.
❾ HIPPODROME
Parts of the huge chariot racing track of ancient
Constantinople, with its columns and obelisk, were
still standing. It was now used as a town square.
❿ PALACE OF IBRAHIM PAŞA
This 16th-century Ottoman palace takes its name
from the grand vizier (chief minister) of Sultan
Suleyman I, "the Magnificent." Paşa was a brilliant
politician, but he was executed in 1536.
⓫ GRAND BAZAAR
This was the largest market in Europe. Each alley
specialized in a particular ware, such as textiles or gold.
⓬ RÜSTEM PAŞA MOSQUE
Built by Sinan in about 1563, this mosque is famous for
its beautiful tiles, made in the Turkish town of Iznik.

13 SÜLEYMANIYE MOSQUE
In this mosque are the tombs of Suleyman the Magnificent and Roxelana.

14 FATIH MOSQUE
This mosque on the site of the Church of the Holy Apostles was built here for Mehmed II in 1463–1470.

15 KIRKÇEŞME WATER SYSTEM
Mimar Sinan built on Byzantine engineering to create the sophisticated Kırkçeşme water system. It was one of the great engineering achievements of the age and relied on precise mathematical calculations.

16 OLD PALACE (ESKI SARAY)
Completed in 1457, this smaller palace was used by the Ottoman court until the new Topkapi Palace was built.

17 BEYAZIT II MOSQUE
This mosque complex, completed in 1506, was built near the ruins of the ancient forum of Theodosius. Its religious school or medrese 18 (today's museum of

calligraphy) was built in 1508.

19 TEKFUR PALACE
The ruins of the former Byzantine Palace of the Porphyrogenitus housed the sultan's private zoo.

20 THEODOSIAN WALLS
After the city walls were blasted by cannons in the siege of 1453, the victorious Ottomans repaired them.

21 FORTRESS OF THE SEVEN TOWERS
When the Ottomans took Constantinople, a section of the walls and the Golden Gate were incorporated into this massive fortress, later a notorious dungeon.

22 YENIKAPI HARBOR
This busy seaport and shipyard was near the ancient harbor of Theodosius.

23 GOLDEN HORN
As well as being the main harbor of the city, this estuary was also the location of the 24 Imperial Arsenal, where warships were built.

25 NEW CITY (BEYOGLÜ OR GALATA)
The north shore of the Golden Horn was populated by foreign traders, many of them Jewish or Greek.

26 GALATA TOWER
This stone tower was built in 1348 by settlers from Italy who lived in Galata at this time.

27 ARAB MOSQUE
This unusual mosque was originally a Christian church built in 1325 for Dominican friars.

28 MAIDEN'S TOWER
The maiden in this tower's name was a legendary princess who died of a snakebite. In the 17th century this tower was a lighthouse.

29 SOUTH OF THE GOLDEN HORN
On the eastern bank of the Bosporus, there were markets, houses, and cemeteries. The Mihrimah Sultan Mosque was commissioned by Suleyman the Magnificent's daughter, Mihrimah Sultan.

CONSTANTINOPLE
550 CE

Rome was reborn in the East.

❶ HAGIA EIRENE
The Church of Holy Peace is the oldest Christian site in Constantinople. Built in the 4th century CE, it burned down in riots in 532 CE and was rebuilt in 548.

❷ COLUMN OF THE GOTHS
Erected in the 3rd or 4th century CE, this Roman column commemorated a victory over a Germanic people called the Goths.

❸ HAGIA SOPHIA
The Church of the Holy Wisdom was the third church on this site and was mostly built in 532–537 CE. It is an architectural masterpiece.

❹ AUGUSTAION
Constantinople's large market square, the Augustaion, was in front of Hagia Sophia.

❺ COLUMN OF JUSTINIAN
This tall column was raised in 543 CE to honor Emperor Justinian's victories. On the top was a statue of the emperor on horseback.

❻ BATHS OF ZEUXIPPOS
Bathhouses have been part of daily life in Istanbul since Roman times. These public baths, famous for their lavish statues, dated back to the 2nd century CE.

❼ GREAT PALACE
Constantinople's magnificent Great Palace complex included reception halls, churches, gardens, a famous golden throne room, and the beautiful **❽** Boukoleon Palace, which was approached from the sea.

❾ CHURCH OF SERGIUS AND BACCHUS
This church was built between 527 and 536 CE in a style that inspired the architecture of Hagia Sophia.

❿ HIPPODROME
This famous chariot racing track was built by Septimius Severus in 203 CE. In 324 CE, it was expanded by Constantine. The fans of each racing team had their own colors. Their support often boiled over into disputes, including the Nika riots of 532 CE.

⓫ MESE
The main street of Constantinople was 82 ft./25 m wide and lined with monuments and shops. It was the route of royal and religious processions.

⓬ PALACE OF MAGNAURA
This was one of the meeting places of the Senate. It lay to the east of the Augustaion.

⓭ MILION
A double arch with a golden dome on top, the Milion was the point from which all distances in the Byzantine Empire were measured.

14 FORUM OF CONSTANTINE
This circular forum in the city center held a column topped by a statue of Constantine as the god Apollo.

15 FORUM OF THEODOSIUS
Previously called the Forum of the Bull, this was rebuilt with churches, baths, and a triumphal column.

16 VALENS AQUEDUCT
The 100-foot-/30-meter-high arches of this aqueduct were part of a larger water network. The Valens system brought water from Thrace, 150 mi./240 km from Istanbul.

17 CHURCH OF THE HOLY APOSTLES
Built in 330 CE and rebuilt in 550 CE, this church was second only to Hagia Sophia in its importance.

18 CHORA CHURCH
This church was first built as part of a monastery.

19 20 21 CISTERNS
Water was kept in underground reservoirs, which were known as cisterns.

22 CONSTANTINE'S WALL
The walls and towers that defended Constantine's city were soon outgrown, but despite earthquake damage over the years, they were left standing.

23 WALLS OF THEODOSIUS
The great walls, towers, and gatehouses of Constantinople were built by Theodosius II in the 5th century. They stretched for 4 mi./6.5 km around the outside of the city. These defenses featured thick inner walls, two layers of outer walls, and a wide moat. They had 96 towers, each around 66 ft./20 m high. The walls were not breached until Constantinople fell to the Ottomans in 1453, when the Ottoman army used enormous cannons to blast through.

24 THE GOLDEN GATE
This marble gate, topped with statues, was the chief ceremonial entrance to the city from the west. It may have been built to celebrate a military victory.

25 STOUDIOS MONASTERY
This monastery opened in 463 CE.

26 HARBOR OF THEODOSIUS
This port, built in the 4th century CE, was one of several on the city's Marmara coast.

27 BOSPORUS
This strait was an important trading route in 500 CE. Constantinople was built at its southern entrance.

28 GOLDEN HORN
The Golden Horn is an estuary that makes a natural harbor for the city. It was protected from attack by sea chains placed across the entrance to stop ships.

29 GALATA
Also known as Peran en Sykais ("the fig field on the other side"), the northern shore of the Golden Horn was a district with its own baths, theater, and forum.

PARIS

Paris rises from the banks of the river Seine, which winds through northern France. It is a city of art, architecture, and fashion — with a stormy history.

PARIS

Country: France
Continent: Europe
Estimated population:
10.9 million (Greater Paris, 2019)
Founded in: 52 BCE as a Roman town
Historic name: Lutetia

WHO HAS LIVED THERE?

Sylvie Guillem (1965–) is one of a long line of famous Parisian ballet dancers. She trained at the Opera Ballet School and went on to become an international star. Her career spanned from 1981 to 2015. Paris has a history of ballet stretching back to the 1660s, and its dancers inspired many famous Parisian artists, such as Edgar Degas.

Marie-Antoinette (1755–1793) was the wife of King Louis XVI. She was known for being out of touch with the harsh realities of life outside the Palace of Versailles. During the French Revolution, Marie-Antoinette was jailed in the grim fortress of the Temple and then at the Conciergerie. She was executed by the guillotine in October 1793.

King Charles V (1338–1380) first ruled France as regent, when his father, Jean II, was captured by the English in 1358. He suppressed the 1356 peasants' revolt and was crowned king in 1364. Charles V set up France's first professional army, and the kingdom prospered under his rule. He is remembered as "Charles the Wise."

PARIS TODAY

The river Seine winds through the center of Paris. High on the medieval cathedral of Notre-Dame, stone gargoyles look out over the Île de la Cité.

On the Right Bank of the Seine is the world's largest art museum, the Louvre. Broad avenues radiate outward from the Arc de Triomphe, a memorial arch, which is France's national monument. On the Left Bank is the student quarter and the soaring iron needle of the Eiffel Tower.

Unlike many other cities, Paris has kept skyscrapers out of its historic center. La Défense, the modern business district, lies 2 mi./3 km to the west of the city.

Paris has been famous as a center of the arts since the Impressionists painted here in the mid-1800s, and the city's talent for high fashion and fine cooking dates back centuries.

So too do Parisian traditions of radical politics and dissent. The wide boulevards of the 19th century were built to enable rapid troop movement across the city to deal with the many uprisings. From Viking raids to revolutions, the city of Paris has withstood it all.

PARIS 1793

In 1793, Paris was at the center of the French Revolution, a period of social upheaval that lasted until 1799. The Revolution began in Paris and sent shock waves around the world. In the streets of the city, carts carried aristocrats, including King Louis XVI and his queen, Marie-Antoinette, to be publicly executed by the dreaded guillotine.

The causes of the Revolution were financial crisis, food shortages, unfair taxes, and social injustice. The motto of today's French Republic remains that of the Revolution—Liberty, Equality, and Fraternity.

The uprising spiraled out of control between 1793 and 1794 and became known as the "Reign of Terror." Mobs of armed men and women roamed the streets wearing the tricolor cockade (a rosette of red, white, and blue). Churches were also attacked, shut down, and often turned into warehouses.

Only 100 years before the French Revolution, Paris had been a city of powerful kings. Louis XIV, the "Sun King," ruled over a glittering court at the Palace of Versailles. The extravagance of the French court was to become one of the main causes of the Revolution.

PARIS 1380

In 1380 King Charles V died. His reign had brought prosperity and some success in the endless conflicts with England known as the Hundred Years' War (1337–1453).

At the time, Paris was a walled city of timbered houses, built even on the tops of the bridges. The medieval royal palace and fortress of Paris was on the Île de la Cité, where the cathedral of Notre-Dame was also built between 1163 and 1345. Paris was an important river port, and a medieval merchant ship still appears on the city's coat of arms today.

In 1380, students from all over Europe came to the city to study. The University of Paris had become the biggest cultural and scientific center in Europe, attracting over 20,000 students each year.

Clovis I, king of the Franks, had made the city his capital in the 6th century. But long before that, Roman invaders built a town on the Left Bank, called Lutetia. They fought off a tribe of Gauls (an Iron Age people from west-central Europe) here in 52 BCE. They were called the Parisii and are the people from whom the city takes its name.

FIND THE RED FLAG TO BEGIN YOUR TOUR OF THIS CITY IN LAYERS.

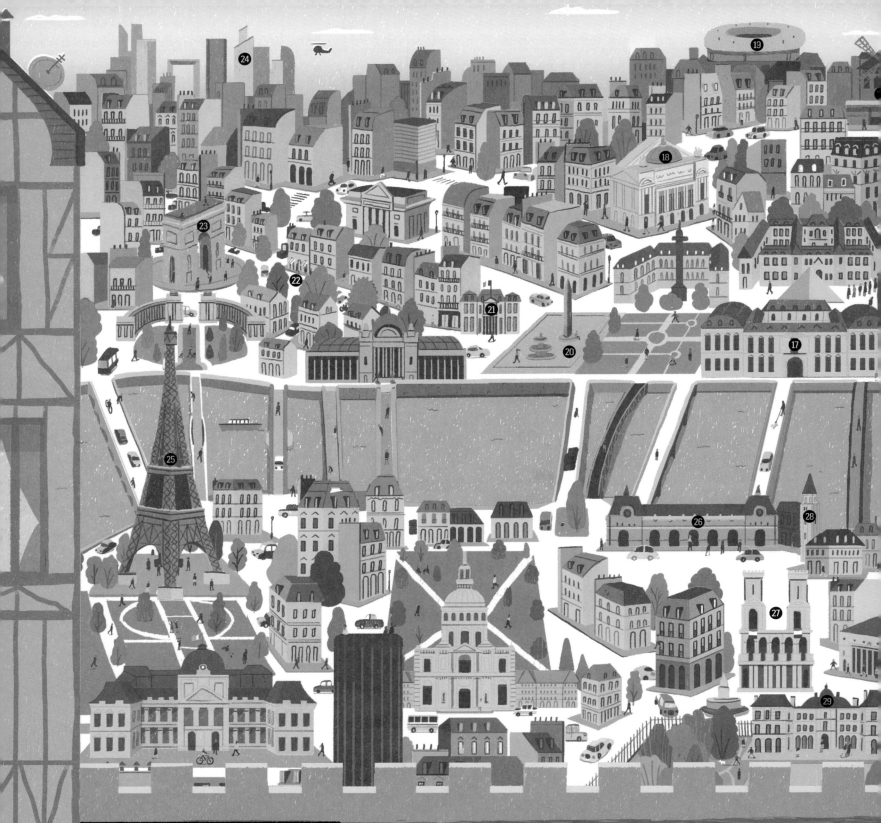

PARIS TODAY

From its wide boulevards to
its ancient cathedrals, Paris remains
a city steeped in history.

❶ NOTRE-DAME DE PARIS
This cathedral is famous for its towers and colorful
stained glass. In 2019, it was badly damaged by a
devastating fire. Restoration is ongoing.

❷ HÔTEL-DIEU DE PARIS
A hospital was founded here in 651 CE. Today it is the
oldest hospital in the city.

❸ SAINTE-CHAPELLE
The old royal chapel still stands within a former
medieval palace.

❹ HÔTEL DE VILLE
The medieval city hall of Paris has been rebuilt

several times — most recently in 1874.

❺ MUSÉE PICASSO
The Spanish artist Pablo Picasso first came to Paris
in 1900 and became part of the city's vibrant art scene.

❻ PLACE DE LA BASTILLE
This square is named after the large fortress
destroyed during the French Revolution.

❼ OPÉRA BASTILLE
This theater is the home of the Paris National Opera.

❽ PLACE DE LA RÉPUBLIQUE
This large square contains a statue of Marianne,
the Goddess of Liberty and a symbol of the French
Republic. She holds an olive branch in her hand.

❾ PHILHARMONIE DE PARIS
An ultramodern performance hall, the Philharmonie de
Paris opened in 2015 in the northeast of the city.

❿ BASILICA OF SAINT-DENIS
This medieval church, 6 mi./9 km to the north of the

city center, was the burial place of French kings.

⓫ MONTMARTRE
This area was the birthplace of Impressionism, one of
the most celebrated art styles around the world.

⓬ SACRÉ-COEUR
This white-domed church is perched on the highest
spot in Paris, with spectacular views over the city.

⓭ MOULIN ROUGE
This 1889 cabaret is the home of the cancan, an
exciting dance with high kicks and cartwheels.

⓮ GARE DU NORD
This railway station is the busiest in Europe.

⓯ CENTRE POMPIDOU
Built in the 1970s, the modern design of the Pompidou
shocked many people of the time. Today it is a
museum of modern art.

⓰ LE FORUM DES HALLES
Once the main food market for Paris, Les Halles

was replaced by a huge shopping center in 1979.

17 LOUVRE MUSEUM
A former royal palace, the Louvre is now the world's largest art museum. It contains Leonardo da Vinci's famous painting the *Mona Lisa*.

18 PALAIS GARNIER
The Palais Garnier was completed in 1875. Today it is used for ballet performances.

19 STADE DE FRANCE
The national stadium of France is used for a variety of events, including rugby and athletic competitions.

20 PLACE DE LA CONCORDE
The biggest square in the city contains statues, fountains, and a towering obelisk from ancient Egypt.

21 ÉLYSÉE PALACE
Finished in 1722, this is the residence of French presidents.

22 AVENUE DES CHAMPS-ÉLYSÉES
This broad avenue is used for grand military parades.

23 ARC DE TRIOMPHE
Since 1836, this arch has commemorated French soldiers. It is the meeting place of 12 wide avenues.

24 LA DÉFENSE
The chief business center of Paris lies 2 mi./3 km to the west of the city proper.

25 EIFFEL TOWER
This iron tower is 1,063 ft./324 m high and was the world's tallest structure when it opened in 1889.

26 MUSÉE D'ORSAY
This museum houses a collection of French paintings, including works by many great Impressionists.

27 THE CHURCH OF SAINT-SULPICE
This church dates back to 1781 and is the second largest church in Paris.

28 SAINT-GERMAIN-DES-PRÉS
The present church is part of an ancient abbey, rebuilt in stone and dedicated in 1163 .

29 PALAIS DE LUXEMBOURG
The French Senate meets in this 17th-century palace.

30 SORBONNE UNIVERSITY
A world-renowned university was founded in Paris in 1257. It still attracts thousands of students to this day.

31 PONT NEUF
Today 37 bridges cross the river Seine. Pont Neuf, meaning "new bridge," is the oldest.

32 MUSÉE DE CLUNY
This museum is inside a building belonging to the abbots of Cluny and celebrates the Middle Ages. The building was inspired by the Pantheon in Rome.

33 PANTHÉON
This state mausoleum honors the memory of some of the great citizens of France.

34 ARÈNES DE LUTÈCE
In 1869 this Roman amphitheater was discovered under the city. It could have seated 17,000 people.

PARIS 1793

By 1793, the flag of the French Revolution could be seen throughout the city.

❶ NOTRE-DAME DE PARIS
When revolutionaries rebelled against the Church, the cathedral was used as a food store. During this time, statues were broken and the central spire came down.

❷ HÔTEL-DIEU DE PARIS
The ancient hospital caught fire in 1772.

❸ SAINTE-CHAPELLE
The revolutionaries rebelled against the idea that kings had a God-given right to rule. During this period revolutionaries raided the royal chapel of the old palace.

❹ PALAIS DE LA CITÉ
From September 1793, revolutionary tribunals were held in the great hall of this medieval palace.

❺ CONCIERGERIE
This part of the Palais de la Cité served as a prison. Marie-Antoinette was held here in 1793.

❻❼ BRIDGES OF THE SEINE
In this year there were two bridges across the Seine renamed by the revolutionaries. The new Pont Louis XV became ❻ the Pont de la Révolution. Pont Royal became ❼ the Pont National.

❽ HÔTEL DE VILLE
During the Revolution this was the meeting place of the Commune, which governed Paris.

❾ BASTILLE RUINS
The medieval prison and fortress was stormed by revolutionaries in 1789 and was eventually destroyed.

❿ LE TEMPLE
During this time the fortress was used as a prison, and the French royal family was held here in 1792.

⓫ BASILICA OF SAINT-DENIS
The abbey where the French kings were buried was vandalized in 1793, during the Revolution.

⓬ ⓭ TRIUMPHAL ARCHES
In the 1600s, two triumphal arches, ⓬ the Porte Saint-Martin and ⓭ Porte Saint-Denis, were commissioned by Louis XIV to honor his military victories.

⓮ LES HALLES
This was once the main food market for Paris. It was built on the site of an old cemetery.

⓯ GRAND CHÂTELET
This medieval stronghold had been a center of law enforcement and a jail under royal rule. Its powers were taken away in 1790, and it was later demolished.

⓰ LOUVRE MUSEUM
It was during the Revolution that this royal palace, the Louvre, became a museum. It displayed art seized from the royal family and church collections.

PARIS 1380

The medieval city was a center of learning, visited by students from all over Europe.

1 NOTRE-DAME DE PARIS
This great cathedral was built between 1163 and 1345. It towered over the Île de la Cité. The statues on the grand porch were originally painted in color.

2 HÔTEL-DIEU DE PARIS
In 1380, this hospital and care home beside the river Seine was already seven centuries old.

3 SAINTE-CHAPELLE
This chapel was built between 1242 and 1248. It housed a holy relic, said to be Jesus's crown of thorns.

4 PALAIS DE LA CITÉ
The original palace of the French kings had impressive stone towers and a clock tower. The building included courts of justice and a prison. In 1358, the palace was invaded during an uprising by the merchants of Paris.

5 PETIT PONT
There has been a bridge in this location since ancient times. This design dated from 1175.

6 PONT SAINT-MICHEL
This stone bridge was built between 1378 and 1387. It was named after the nearby chapel of Saint-Michel.

7 PONT AUX MEUNIERS
This footbridge between the Right Bank and the Île de la Cité had floating waterwheels moored between its arches for grinding grain.

8 PONT AU CHANGE
This was a wooden bridge named after moneylenders and goldsmiths. Many of the wooden bridges over the Seine had houses built on them.

9 PONT DES PLANCHES DE MILBRAY
This small bridge was built to replace the Grand-Pont, the original Seine crossing. It was destroyed by floods in 1406.

10 LE GRAND CHÂTELET
This stone fortress guarded access to the Île de la Cité via the Pont au Change. It later became a prison.

11 ST. MARTIN-DES-CHAMPS
The ancient priory was an influential monastery established in what is now the center of Paris. Many of its buildings survive to this day and are considered treasures of medieval architecture.

12 MAISON AUX PILIERS
In 1357, the city hall of Paris moved to this site. The original building was eventually destroyed by a fire.

13 BASTILLE
Bastille Saint-Antoine was an enormous fortress built to defend the city from English attacks during the

14 LE TEMPLE
Originally a base for the Knights Templar, this fortress became a treasury and later a prison.

15 BASILICA OF SAINT-DENIS
Medieval pilgrims traveled to this abbey and church, built to the north of Paris in 1144. King Charles V and Queen Jeanne de Bourbon were buried here.

16 LES HALLES
Market stalls were set up in the fields beside the Holy Innocents' Cemetery. Covered halls were added in 1183.

17 LOUVRE CASTLE
In 1190, King Philip II built a castle with a moat as part of the city's defenses. King Charles V converted it into a royal palace from 1364 to 1380.

18 SAINT-GERMAIN-DES-PRÉS
This abbey had been rebuilt in stone in 1044. It became an important center of learning.

19 CITY WALLS
The walls of Charles V on the Right Bank of the Seine were built between 1356 and 1383. The Left Bank still had the earlier walls of Philip II.

20 TOUR DE NESLE
This stone tower, built around 1200, was part of the city defenses on the Left Bank. It stood directly opposite the Louvre Castle.

21 HÔTEL SAINT-POL
Charles V spent much of his time at this new royal residence, completed in 1364. It was later destroyed by fire.

22 LE PETIT CHÂTELET
This stronghold gatehouse on the Left Bank guarded access to the Île de la Cité via the Petit Pont.

23 SAINT-SÉVERIN
This Gothic church dates back to the 13th century. Today the bell tower houses the oldest bell in Paris.

24 COLLÈGE DES BERNARDINS
From 1248 this was a center for Cistercian monks studying at the University of Paris. The Cistercians followed the teachings of a great reformer called St. Bernard of Clairvaux (1090–1153).

25 ABBEY OF ST. GENEVIEVE
This abbey and its large library was a center of learning within the old University of Paris.

26 HÔTEL DE CLUNY
In 1334, the monks of Cluny built a residence, a church, and a college on the Left Bank.

27 SORBONNE UNIVERSITY
A college was founded here in 1257 as part of the University of Paris. Students came to the city from all over Europe, using Latin as a common language. To this day, the district is known as the Latin Quarter.

BEIJING

This former city of emperors now dominates the world once more as an economic hub and the capital of the People's Republic of China.

BEIJING

Country: People's Republic of China
Continent: Asia
Estimated population: 21 million (2018)
Founded in: around the 11th century BCE
Historic names: Beiping, Dadu, Yanjing, Khanbaliq, Zhongdu, Jicheng

WHO HAS LIVED THERE?

Zhang Huoding (1971–) is a star of Beijing opera, a type of theater that dates back to the 1790s. She is best known for her role as Xue Xiangling in *The Jewelry Purse*. Beijing opera is famous for its lavish costumes, dramatic makeup, and stylized movement.

Sun Yat-sen and Song Qingling (Sun 1866–1925; Song 1893–1981). Sun was a leader in the revolutionary movement that overthrew imperial rule in China. He was briefly president of the republic and died in 1925. He is honored as the father of modern China. Sun's wife was also politically active during this period.

The **Jiajing Emperor** (1507–1567) ruled in the 16th century. Known for his cruelty, he survived an assassination attempt from 16 women in the Imperial Palace in 1542. After this he refused to live in the Forbidden City. He spent much of his time trying to learn how to live forever, but is thought to have been poisoned by one of his own potions.

BEIJING TODAY

Beijing was once ruled by powerful emperors. Today this sprawling city balances its ancient past with its present as a modern metropolis.

Beijing has grown rapidly over the last 20 years. In 2019, it was the world's sixth largest city and the second biggest in China after Shanghai. The People's Republic of China has the world's second largest economy, and visitors flock to see the city's architecture and modern technology. Since Beijing hosted the 2008 Olympic Games, the city's skyline has become crowded with futuristic skyscrapers and stadiums.

Beijing has had a turbulent history. Uprisings, foreign armies, modernization, and political turmoil in the 1960s destroyed much of the old city. However, glimpses of Beijing's ancient past still survive to fascinate visitors. At the heart of Beijing is the Forbidden City, where the former Imperial Palace still stands behind high red walls. Ornate temples and traditional buildings can be seen throughout the city. To the north, the Great Wall of China snakes its way over hillsides, and the sight attracts millions of visitors each year.

BEIJING 1912

In 1912 Nationalist leader Sun Yat-sen declared China a republic after 1,132 years of imperial rule. The power of the emperors had been weakened over many years by invaders seizing control of ports and trade and by political unrest. The last imperial ruler, Emperor Puyi, was only six years old when he was forced to abdicate.

In 1900, Beijing saw bitter fighting between Western forces and the Chinese rebels called the "Boxers." By 1912 many of the traditional buildings and temples had fallen into disrepair. Western-style buildings such as banks, churches, and embassies began to appear in the foreigners' district, which was known as the Legation Quarter.

Traditional clothing was still common during this period, and many men wore their hair in a long pigtail (known as a queue), a legal requirement under the old Qing emperors. Life in the siheyuans — traditional homes built around courtyards — was often overcrowded. People shared water and food, but working people were poor and many went hungry.

BEIJING 1553

In 1553 China was ruled by the Jiajing Emperor of the Ming dynasty. Beijing was a series of walled cities, each with its own social class, beliefs, and trades.

At its center was the Forbidden City, which the public could not enter. This stood inside the Imperial City, with its beautiful parks and goldfish ponds. This in turn was surrounded by the Inner City, which contained painted temples, monasteries, gateways, and towers.

A busy Outer City was also growing in the south, with new walls completed in 1553. The most important buildings faced south, to honor the sun.

During the Ming dynasty, the Great Wall of China was rebuilt and strengthened. This period also saw the restoration of the Grand Canal, the longest man-made waterway on Earth at 1,100 mi./1,770 km long. It enabled the transportation of food and goods to the capital.

Beijing, under various names, already had an ancient history. In 1215 invading Mongols had rebuilt their capital here, which they called Dadu. Even before the Chinese empire was founded, the Zhou dynasty had thrived here. They founded Beijing over 3,000 years ago and named it Jicheng.

BEIJING TODAY

Beijing is a busy metropolis where glittering skyscrapers stand alongside ancient temples.

❶ IMPERIAL PALACE MUSEUM
This once Forbidden City, surrounded by a moat and high walls, offers a glimpse of the old Chinese empire. The complex attracts millions of visitors each year and is filled with gardens and painted temples.

❷ HALL OF SUPREME HARMONY
This hall was the chief throne room of the emperors. The other two ceremonial centers were the Hall of Preserving Harmony and the Hall of Central Harmony.

❸ IMPERIAL ANCESTRAL TEMPLE
This famous temple stands just to the east of the Forbidden City. In the past, ceremonies were held there to honor the emperors' ancestors.

❹ BEIHAI PARK
This popular park was originally part of the old Imperial City gardens. The white tower, or dagoba, is a Buddhist shrine.

❺ NATIONAL AQUATICS CENTRE
Another reminder of the 2008 Olympics, this "Water Cube" is now an aquatics leisure center.

❻ NATIONAL STADIUM
This sports stadium became famous as the "Bird's Nest" during the 2008 Olympic Games.

❼ SUMMER PALACE
The emperors used this palace to escape from the heat of the city in the summer months. Today it is a popular tourist spot, surrounded by lakes and parks.

❽ NATIONAL LIBRARY OF CHINA
This national library holds 35 million items in its collection. It is the largest library in China.

❾ ZIZHUYUAN PARK
The "Purple Bamboo Park" includes three lakes, hills, and gardens. It is renowned for its bamboo scenery.

❿ MEI LANFANG GRAND THEATRE
Traditional Beijing opera is popular throughout China. This theater is named after one of Beijing's famous opera stars, Mei Lanfang (1894–1961).

⓫ BEIJING ZOO
This is a very popular zoo and research center. Its main attraction is the panda house.

⓬ SIHEYUAN
The traditional courtyard housing of Beijing can still be seen today in some districts of the city.

⓭ MILLENNIUM MONUMENT
Commemorating the year 2000, this large complex includes a monument and Beijing's World Art Museum.

⓮ BEIJING CAPITAL MUSEUM
This museum celebrates the history of Beijing. Its

collection includes ancient writings and paintings.

⑮ WHITE CLOUD TEMPLE
Taoist temples have stood on this site for over 13 centuries. The entrance is marked by an ornate three-arched gateway.

⑯ NATIONAL CENTRE FOR PERFORMING ARTS
Known as the "Giant Egg," this domed building shows ballet, theater, and opera performances.

⑰ GREAT HALL OF THE PEOPLE
This 1959 building is where the National People's Congress assembles to pass laws.

⑱ TIANANMEN SQUARE
This huge square was enlarged in 1954 and today is often used for parades. The People's Republic of China was proclaimed here in 1949.

⑲ XIANNONGTAN (TEMPLE OF AGRICULTURE)
Xiannongtan is a popular tourist spot filled with halls and altars. It was here that the emperors performed ancient farming rituals and ceremonies.

⑳ XIANNONGTAN STADIUM
This sports stadium is mostly used for soccer games.

㉑ TIANTAN (TEMPLE OF HEAVEN)
In this popular park you can find ancient ritual halls, marble platforms, and the Hall of Prayer for Good Harvests.

㉒ MING CITY WALL RUINS PARK
This park holds the remains of sections of the old city wall and the watchtower, Dongbianmen.

㉓ CHAOYANG
This is Beijing's modern business and cultural district.

㉔ ㉕ GUOZIJIAN AND CONFUCIUS TEMPLE
The Guozijian was the old imperial college, a center of learning from ancient times. It can be found by the temple of Confucius, which dates back to 1302.

㉖ ANCIENT OBSERVATORY
Ancient Chinese astronomers made many important discoveries. There were observatories in Beijing as early as the 1200s, and this one was built in 1442.

㉗ 798 ART ZONE
This former industrial area was taken over by contemporary artists in the 1990s and has become famous for its cutting-edge art.

㉘ CHINA WORLD TRADE CENTER
This 81-story tower offers fantastic views of the city from its observation deck.

㉙ RING ROADS
Beijing has six distinctive ring roads that surround the city. The roads mimic the shape of the old city walls.

㉚ GALAXY SOHO
This enormous complex is the largest shopping center in Beijing. It is filled with restaurants and luxury shops.

㉛ GREAT WALL OF CHINA
Built between 770 BCE and 1633, this ancient wall is more than 12,500 mi./20,000 km long.

BEIJING 1912

The 1911 Revolution saw the fall of the last Chinese dynasty after more than 2,000 years of imperial rule.

❶ IMPERIAL PALACE
After the revolution, the Forbidden City remained the home of the former emperor, Puyi. Many imperial treasures were stolen and sold.

❷ HALL OF SUPREME HARMONY
During this period, revolutionaries dismantled the emperor's throne and damaged many important halls.

❸ IMPERIAL ANCESTRAL TEMPLE
Under the new republic, this temple would become a museum, surrounded by a public park.

❹ IMPERIAL CITY
In 1912 the Republican government took over the area surrounding the Imperial Palace. This city still had its own walls, but many of the moats were running dry.

❺ BEIHAI PARK
In 1912 the fabulous gardens, lakes, and temples of Beihai Park came under government control.

❻ ZHONGNANHAI GARDENS
Yuan Shikai, who became the first president of the Republic of China in 1912, set up his presidential palace in the gardens of the Imperial City.

❼❽ DRUM AND BELL TOWERS
These two towers were built to mark the passing of the hours in the ancient city. They were restored in 1911, but no longer had a practical use for timekeeping.

❾ BEIJING UNIVERSITY
In 1898 an Imperial University was founded on this site, and in 1912 it was renamed the Government University of Beijing. It went on to become a great center of learning and political debate.

❿ XIZHIMEN STATION
Today known as Beijing North, this railway station was originally built in 1905. The railway became a symbol of changing times in China.

⓫ SUMMER PALACE
The Summer Palace was badly damaged by European troops in 1860 and again in 1900. It was opened to the public in 1914.

⓬ SIHEYUAN
In 1912 the traditional courtyard housing and narrow lanes of ancient Beijing still covered much of the city.

⓭ WHITE CLOUD TEMPLE
As the center of the Chinese philosophy of Taoism, this temple still flourished behind its ornate gateway.

⓮ NIUJIE MOSQUE
This is the oldest mosque in Beijing, built in 996 CE. It survived the upheavals of the 20th century and was renovated several times.

⑮ TEMPLE OF AGRICULTURE

This temple was last used for the imperial farming rituals in 1906. Then it was used by the army before being restored to its former glory.

⑯ ZHENGYANGMEN RAILWAY

Built in 1906, this was Beijing's first railway station.

⑰ TIANANMEN GATE

In 1912, the "Gate of Heavenly Peace" still guarded the approach to the Meridian Gate of the Forbidden City.

⑱ TIANANMEN SQUARE

During this period, this large square covered a much smaller area than it does today. Official buildings around the square had also been greatly damaged during the Boxer Rebellion.

⑲ GATE OF CHINA

This ceremonial gateway was renamed the Gate of China in 1912. It occupied much of the area taken up today by Tiananmen Square until its demolition in 1954.

⑳ TIANTAN

The Temple of Heaven was badly damaged in 1900 by international armed forces, who used it as a command post.

㉑ INNER CITY WALLS

The Inner City walls were still standing in 1912 and traditional merchant caravans of Bactrian camels still passed through the gates. By the 1930s they had been knocked down to make way for rail and road traffic.

㉒ LEGATION QUARTER

In 1912 this area was filled with Western hospitals, banks, hotels, and embassies. Legation residents did not have to obey Chinese laws.

㉓ NATIONAL ASSEMBLY HALL

China's first elections were held here in 1912, but the assembly hall was only used from time to time in the troubled decade that followed.

㉔ ANCIENT OBSERVATORY

Precious historical instruments from the Ancient Observatory were looted by French and German troops in 1900, but were later returned to the site.

㉕ CONFUCIUS TEMPLE

This ancient temple was still standing in 1912, but was damaged during the 1966 Cultural Revolution.

㉖ DONGYUE MIAO

This Taoist temple would be attacked in the 1960s, but was restored to its former glory in 2002.

㉗ GRAND HOTEL OF PEKING

The oldest and most famous hotel in Beijing opened its doors to guests in 1915. It became a favorite of travelers to the city.

BEIJING 1553

In 1553, Beijing was a city of towering walls, forbidden palaces, and ornate temples.

❶ IMPERIAL PALACE
Not yet known as the Forbidden City, this palace complex was built between 1406 and 1420. It was the center of imperial power in China for five centuries.

❷ HALL OF SUPREME HARMONY
The largest of palace halls, this is where emperors sat on the throne to discuss matters of state.

❸ IMPERIAL ANCESTRAL TEMPLE
Honoring one's ancestors was an important Chinese tradition. The spectacular halls of this ancestral temple were completed in 1420.

❹ IMPERIAL CITY WALLS
The high walls and moats of the Imperial Palace were surrounded by an area called the Imperial City. This too was moated, with high walls and seven gates.

❺ MERIDIAN GATE
Emperors would survey troops and carry out important ceremonies from the top of the enormous gate.

❻ XIYUAN PARK
An imperial pleasure garden called Xiyuan was laid out in the Imperial City in the 1400s. It included three lakes known as Beihai, Zhonghai, and Nanhai.

❼ ZIZHUYUAN
Artificial lakes were created here in the 1100s. Emperors loved to rearrange the landscape around the city, creating hills, canals, pavilions, and pleasure gardens.

❽ JINGSHAN HILL
This man-made hill was made from soil excavated during the building of the Imperial Palace moat. The

court would enjoy the view from the hilltop pavilions.

❾ ❿ DRUM AND BELL TOWERS
These towers (Gulou and Zhonglou) were built to mark the passing of time with drums and bells. They were built in 1273 and rebuilt twice due to fires.

⓫ INNER CITY WALLS
About 15 mi./24 km of walls defended the Inner City during the Ming dynasty. There were nine gates in the 1500s, protected by many watchtowers.

⓬ SHISANLING (THE MING TOMBS)
About 30 mi./50 km north of Beijing are the tombs of 13 Ming dynasty emperors, dating from 1420 to 1644. They are still standing today.

⓭ TEMPLE OF THE MOON
This temple was built by the Jiajing Emperor in 1530. Here the emperor made offerings to the moon.

⓮ WHITE CLOUD TEMPLE
Taoism was one of three main religions of China,

42

alongside Confucianism and Buddhism. By 1553 there had been Taoist temples on this site for 800 years.

⑮ IMPERIAL ELEPHANT STABLES
Elephants were kept in the imperial stables until around 1900 and were often used for ceremonies.

⑯ TIANANMEN
In 1420 the "Gate of Heavenly Peace" was built as a ceremonial arch, but it burned down after a lightning strike. It was rebuilt in 1465 and became the main gate leading from the Inner City into the Imperial City.

⑰ ZHENGYANGMEN GATE
The main gate to the Inner City was built in 1419 and from 1439 included a barbican called the Arrow Tower.

⑱ TEMPLE OF AGRICULTURE
At the spring equinox, each emperor would lead a procession from the Imperial Palace to this temple. There the emperor would put on farmer's clothes and perform a plowing ceremony.

⑲ DAMINGMEN
This was a long ceremonial gateway situated south of Tiananmen, where Mao Zedong's mausoleum is today.

⑳ TIANTAN
As Chinese emperors were hailed as "Sons of Heaven," the Temple of Heaven was seen as a very important site. In 1530, the Jiajing Emperor added a great circular mound to the south of the Great Sacrificial Hall.

㉑ OUTER CITY WALLS
In 1553, Beijing had expanded beyond the Inner City walls. A new defensive wall had been constructed that would protect the outer districts.

㉒ GRAND CANAL
The Grand Canal was restored during the 1400s. It stretched over 1,100 mi./1,770 km and opened up trading routes with the rest of China.

㉓ TEMPLE OF THE SUN
This temple was a Taoist altar built by the Jiajing

Emperor, who was a strong opponent of Buddhism.

㉔ DONGYUE MIAO
This Taoist temple and its courtyards were originally built in the 1300s.

㉕ CONFUCIUS TEMPLE
Built in 1302, this temple was dedicated to the philosopher Confucius (551–479 BCE). His teachings formed one of the three great beliefs of ancient China.

㉖ GUOZIJIAN
At the Imperial College, students could study law, mathematics, archery, and calligraphy.

㉗ TEMPLE OF EARTH
Ditan was a Taoist temple built by the Jiajing Emperor in 1530. The emperor was known to be devoted to this religion, but often neglected his state duties.

㉘ GREAT WALL OF CHINA
During the Ming dynasty, the Great Wall of China was rebuilt and strengthened.

LONDON

Blue skies or rain? London changes its look with the seasons. This great city has stood on the banks of the river Thames for nearly 2,000 years.

LONDON

Country: United Kingdom
Continent: Europe
Estimated population: 9.2 million (2019)
Founded in: around 43 CE as a Roman town
Historic names: Londinium, Lundenwic

WHO HAS LIVED THERE?

Queen Elizabeth II (b. 1926–) is the longest ruling monarch in British history. Her reign, which began in 1952, has seen many social and political changes affecting London and Britain's role in the wider world. The queen's London home is at Buckingham Palace. When the royal flag is flying above the palace, it shows that she is at home.

Queen Victoria (1819–1901) ruled over Britain when the British Empire was at the height of its power. London was a center of the new industrial age, and shipping brought valuable cargo here from all over Britain's global empire. Victoria was married to a German prince called Albert, and their children married into royal families across Europe.

William Shakespeare (1564–1616) was a playwright, actor, and poet. He was born in Stratford-upon-Avon but made his name in London during the 1590s. His group of players founded the Globe Theatre on the South Bank of the Thames. His plays included comedies, tragedies, and histories. They are still read and performed all over the world.

LONDON TODAY

London, in the southeast of England, is the capital city of the United Kingdom. Londoners have their origins in many parts of the world, and this has always been an exciting, lively, and multicultural city.

The oldest part of London is the business district, known simply as "the City." Here you will find the great cathedral of St. Paul's, founded in 604 CE. The dome of the cathedral that stands today is dwarfed by gleaming skyscrapers.

In the Middle Ages, a second city grew up to the west at Westminster, now home of the United Kingdom's parliament, and these twin cities soon merged.

Modern London is huge, taking in the shopping and entertainment district of the West End, street markets, city squares, palaces, museums, galleries, and leafy green parks. Transport includes red double-decker buses, sturdy black taxis, and the Underground, also known as "the Tube."

LONDON 1863

In 1863, London was the center of the British Empire, ruled over by Queen Victoria. Ships from all over the world docked by the river Thames, downstream from London Bridge. The river was smelly in those days and polluted with sewage.

Barges carried coal for homes and for the factories of the new industrial age. Chimneys filled the air with smoke and soot. The streets were jammed with horse-drawn carriages and carts. Laborers were transforming the city, building

modern sewers, river embankments, railway stations, and the world's first underground rail line.

London's foggy streets were described vividly in the novels of Charles Dickens. They were busy with street sellers, bakers, fishmongers, chimney sweeps, thieves, lawyers, rich merchants, and servants. Wealthy people lived in smart new town houses, but the poor were crowded into run-down slums.

LONDON 1613

About 200,000 people lived in London in the 1600s. In 1603, the throne of England had passed to the King of Scotland, James VI. He now also ruled England as James I. His chief palace was at Whitehall, in Westminster.

London Bridge was the only way to cross the Thames unless you took a boat. These were troubled times and the heads of executed traitors were displayed on the bridge as a warning to would-be rebels.

Most houses were timber-framed, and the spires of churches rose above the rooftops. The cathedral of St. Paul's, built in 1087–1314, towered over the city.

London's best-known theater was the Globe, south of the river. It burned down in 1613 during a performance of

Shakespeare's play *Henry VIII* and was replaced in 1614.

In 1666 a devastating fire would destroy much of the city that had stood in 1613.

London's history goes back many centuries before the 1600s, however. The fortified town of Londinium was established by Roman invaders in 43 CE. It was burned down by Boudicca, rebel queen of the native Iceni tribe, in 60 CE, and was rebuilt. In about 500 CE Anglo-Saxons were settling in Lundenwic, as the city was called then. In the 800s there were attacks by Vikings and in 1066 the Normans invaded. London is a city that has been destroyed many times, but it always reinvents itself.

FIND THE RED FLAG TO BEGIN YOUR TOUR OF THIS CITY IN LAYERS.

LONDON TODAY

This modern city has history around every corner.

① HOUSES OF PARLIAMENT
Today the Palace of Westminster houses the U.K. Parliament. The bell in its clock tower is Big Ben.

② WESTMINSTER ABBEY
Kings and queens are crowned at this great church, which was founded in 1065.

③ 10 DOWNING STREET
This is the home of the U.K.'s prime minister.

④ BUCKINGHAM PALACE
This palace is the London home of the U.K.'s monarch.

⑤ HYDE PARK
One of many large green spaces in the city, this park

is also used for political rallies and concerts.

⑥ ⑦ ⑧ MUSEUMS
London has many impressive museums, including ⑥ the Natural History Museum, ⑦ the Victoria and Albert Museum, and ⑧ the British Museum.

⑨ TRELLICK TOWER
A residential block built in 1972, Trellick Tower is a landmark in the "brutalist" architectural style.

⑩ PICCADILLY CIRCUS
A busy crossroad marked by the Shaftesbury Memorial Fountain and statue (1893), nicknamed "Eros."

⑪ TRAFALGAR SQUARE
This large public square is beside the National Gallery, which is full of wonderful paintings.

⑫ BT TOWER
This communications tower dates from 1965.

⑬ COVENT GARDEN
Once London's fruit and vegetable market, Covent

Garden is now a fashionable area of shops and cafés.

⑭ STAPLE INN
Dating back to 1585, Staple Inn serves as a center of legal practice. It was restored after WWII.

⑮ THE SEVEN STARS
The Seven Stars pub (public house) dates back to 1602 and is thought to be one of the oldest in London.

⑯ ROYAL COURTS OF JUSTICE
The 1882 Royal Courts of Justice stand on Fleet Street, the center of journalism until the 1980s.

⑰ ST. PAUL'S CATHEDRAL
The huge, domed St. Paul's was designed by Sir Christopher Wren as a replacement for the old cathedral, destroyed in the 1666 Great Fire of London.

⑱ THE OLD BAILEY
Atop the Central Criminal Court building, nicknamed the "Old Bailey," is a statue of Lady Justice.

⑲ SMITHFIELD
This has been a meat market for over 800 years.

⑳ 41 CLOTH FAIR, FARRINGDON
Built in 1597–1614, it's the city's oldest surviving home.

㉑ BARBICAN CENTRE
Taking its name from the ancient fortifications of the City, the modern Barbican Centre includes apartment blocks in the brutalist style and an arts center.

㉒ OLD CITY WALLS
Sections of these still stand. The original walls were built by the Romans.

㉓ GUILDHALL
The Guildhall is the town hall of the City of London.

㉔㉕㉖ CITY SKYSCRAPERS
There are many high-rise buildings in the City district. Notable ones include ㉔ the "Walkie-Talkie" (525 ft./160 m), ㉕ the "Cheese Grater" (735 ft./224 m), and ㉖ the "Gherkin" (591 ft./180 m).

㉗ BANK OF ENGLAND
This building was constructed in 1925–1939. In the bank's vaults are over 400,000 gold bars.

㉘ SHOREDITCH
In recent years artists and businesses have moved into this district in the traditionally poor East End.

㉙ TOWER OF LONDON
In this 11th-century stone castle, visitors can explore the dungeons and see the Crown Jewels.

㉚ TOWER BRIDGE
Opened in 1894, this is one of 33 bridges that cross the Thames in Greater London. This bridge opens to let ships sail through.

㉛ THE SHARD
Soaring above London Bridge, the Shard is the U.K.'s tallest building at 1,004 ft./306 m. It opened in 2013.

㉜ SOUTHWARK CATHEDRAL
Parts of this cathedral date back to 1220.

㉝ SHAKESPEARE'S GLOBE
This 1997 building, based on theater design in Shakespeare's time, is near the site of the old Globe.

㉞ TATE MODERN
This exciting gallery of modern art opened in 2000. It is housed in the former Bankside Power Station.

㉟ WINCHESTER PALACE
The ruins of Winchester Palace can still be seen today.

㊱ SOUTH BANK
The South Bank was redeveloped for the 1951 Festival of Britain. It includes the Royal Festival Hall and the National Theatre (1976).

㊲ WATERLOO STATION
This is just one of ten big railway terminals that surround London.

㊳ LONDON EYE
The London Eye (2000) is a gigantic Ferris wheel, 443 ft./135 m high. It was built to celebrate the millennium.

LONDON 1863

The most powerful city on Earth was home to the very rich and very poor.

1 HOUSES OF PARLIAMENT
Most of the old Palace of Westminster burned down in 1834. It was rebuilt in 1840–1870.

2 WESTMINSTER ABBEY
Queen Victoria was crowned at the abbey in 1838. Its western towers date from 1722 and 1745.

3 THE EMBANKMENT
Embankments were built along the north bank of the Thames from 1862. These improved drainage.

4 BUCKINGHAM PALACE
Queen Victoria was the first monarch to live here, but she rarely used it after Prince Albert died in 1861.

5 ST. JAMES'S PALACE
Queen Victoria married Prince Albert here in 1840.

6 HYDE PARK
Fashionable riders exercised their horses along Rotten Row in Hyde Park, and the park also hosted the Great Exhibition of 1851.

7 VICTORIA AND ALBERT MUSEUM
A new museum opened in this location in 1856. It was renamed the Victoria and Albert (or "V&A") in 1899. The 19th-century middle class had more leisure than ever before, and museums offered entertainment and education of growing scientific and cultural knowledge.

8 PADDINGTON STATION
The Metropolitan Railway opened the world's first underground line from here to the City in January 1863.

9 THE NATIONAL GALLERY
The gallery opened in 1838 and houses the national collection of paintings.

10 TRAFALGAR SQUARE
On top of the column in the square is a statue of Admiral Lord Nelson, who won the Battle of Trafalgar, a famous naval battle, in 1805.

11 COVENT GARDEN
The market for fruit and vegetables was built in 1830.

12 BRITISH MUSEUM
This museum first opened in 1759, and today's vast building dates from 1857. In the 1860s, the museum was collecting items from all over the world.

13 14 15 THE STRAND
The old street was being rebuilt, with hotels and a music hall for popular entertainment. Charing Cross railway station **14** would open in 1864, and Somerset House **15** had replaced Somerset Place in 1779.

16 TEMPLE BAR
This arch between Fleet Street and the Strand was famous for creating traffic jams.

17 MIDDLE TEMPLE HALL
Since the Middle Ages, four areas had been centers of the legal profession. These were Middle Temple, Inner Temple, Lincoln's Inn, and Gray's Inn.

18 ST. PAUL'S CATHEDRAL
In 1863, Christopher Wren's cathedral was still the tallest building in London. It would remain so until the BT Tower was built in 1965.

19 OLD BAILEY AND NEWGATE
The criminal courts at the Old Bailey stood beside Newgate, the notorious prison.

20 SMITHFIELD
The old livestock market had moved in 1855, but a new market for the sale of meat was being built. At this time, cows, sheep, and pigs were often seen in the city.

21 OLD CITY WALLS
By the 1800s, most of the old city walls had been destroyed or built into other buildings.

22 ROYAL EXCHANGE
The Royal Exchange was rebuilt in 1844 after a fire.

23 BANK OF ENGLAND
The nation's central bank was founded in 1694. This building by Sir John Soane stood from 1788 to 1925.

24 THE MONUMENT
This 200-foot/62-meter high column with a fiery top marks the start of the 1666 Great Fire of London.

25 MANSION HOUSE
Built between 1739 and 1758, this is the official residence of the lord mayor of the City of London.

26 BILLINGSGATE
The fish market received catches by ship, road, and rail.

27 WILTON'S MUSIC HALL
Music halls, where popular songs were performed, were common. Wilton's opened in 1859.

28 29 SLUMS
In parts of the city like 28 St. Giles and 29 the East

End, there were areas of extreme poverty.

30 NEW LONDON BRIDGE
Old London Bridge had been replaced in 1831.

31 GEORGE INN
This coaching inn dates back hundreds of years. It appears in Charles Dickens's novel *Little Dorrit*.

32 LAMBETH
On the riverside (today's South Bank) were breweries, wharves, and a lead works with a tall shot tower.

33 WATERLOO STATION
This railway terminus opened in 1848. Railways revolutionized travel in the 19th century. In London they encouraged the building of new suburbs.

34 THE RIVER THAMES
The expansion of the British Empire and increased use of the steamship led to chaotic river traffic on the Thames. Between 1800 and 1880 larger, deeper docks were built. Many Londoners worked on or near the river.

LONDON 1613

London was famous for theaters ... and dangerous political plots.

1 HOUSES OF PARLIAMENT
This medieval palace housed Parliament. In the Gunpowder Plot of 1605, conspirators, including Guy Fawkes, had tried to blow up the House of Lords.

2 WESTMINSTER ABBEY
James VI of Scotland was crowned James I of England in the ancient abbey in 1603.

3 WESTMINSTER HALL
The hall was built in 1097, and it was the largest in Europe at the time. It still stands in London today.

4 ST. JAMES'S PALACE
St. James's Palace was built from 1531 to 1536, on the site of a former leper hospital.

5 HYDE PARK
A royal hunting park from 1536, Hyde Park would be opened to the public in 1637.

6 COVENT GARDEN
In the Middle Ages this area had been a "convent garden," supplying produce to the local nuns and to Westminster Abbey. In the 1630s a new square and church would be built here.

7 CHARING CROSS
This cross was erected by King Edward I in 1291–1294 in honor of his wife, Eleanor of Castile. It would be demolished in 1647, during the English Civil War.

8 9 10 PALACES
Along the North Bank of the Thames were grand palaces and gardens. Henry VII founded **8** the Savoy Hospital on the site of another former palace, while **9** Somerset Place was built by the Duke of Somerset from 1547 to 1552. **10** Baynards Castle was turned into a palace by Henry VIII.

11 TEMPLE BAR
An arch stood between the Strand and Fleet Street, marking the outer boundary of the old City of London.

12 MIDDLE TEMPLE HALL
Middle Temple Hall had been completed in 1572, in the lawyers' district. The play *Twelfth Night* by Shakespeare was performed here in 1602.

13 STAPLE INN
Staple Inn, like most of London's buildings in 1613, was made of timber. After the Great Fire of London in 1666, new wooden structures were prohibited.

14 OLD BAILEY AND NEWGATE
A law court at the Old Bailey was already in use in 1585. It was next to Newgate, a medieval prison.

15 THE SEVEN STARS
Public houses called the "Seven Stars" tended to

attract Dutch sailors. The stars stood for the seven provinces of the Netherlands.

⑯ ST. BARTHOLOMEW'S

Part of this medieval priory survived as a church, alongside the famous St. Bartholomew's Hospital.

⑰ SMITHFIELD

This area was a busy livestock market, with drovers bringing cattle into the city.

⑱ 41 CLOTH FAIR, FARRINGDON

At this time, 41 Cloth Fair was a brand-new house.

⑲ GUILDHALL

The city's town hall, built in 1411–1440, was used for public ceremonies and famous state trials, including that of Lady Jane Grey, queen for nine days before she was executed for treason in 1553.

⑳ OLD ST. PAUL'S CATHEDRAL

London's cathedral was built in 1087–1314. Londoners gathered to socialize and trade in the churchyard. The building was destroyed in the Great Fire of 1666.

㉑ CUSTOM HOUSE

Taxes on shipped goods were collected here.

㉒ BILLINGSGATE

This wharf already specialized in selling fish.

㉓ ROYAL EXCHANGE

The original building, known as the Bourse, dated to 1571 and was a place to shop and trade. It was founded by merchant Sir Thomas Gresham.

㉔ CITY WALLS

London had outgrown its city walls before the 1600s, but their gatehouses survived until the 1760s. The walls were first built by the Romans in 200 CE.

㉕ TOWER OF LONDON

The central "White Tower" was built by William the Conqueror in the 1070s. By 1616 it had housed many famous prisoners, including Anne Boleyn (Henry VIII's second wife) and the explorer Sir Walter Raleigh.

㉖ OLD LONDON BRIDGE

From Roman times there was a wooden bridge here. Between 1209 and 1831 a stone bridge linked the City with Southwark. It was lined with shops and houses.

㉗ ST. SAVIOUR'S

Shakespeare's brother Edmund was buried here in 1607. From 1106 to 1538 this church was part of Southwark Priory and monks worshipped here.

㉘ WINCHESTER PALACE

This was the home of the bishops of Winchester.

㉙㉚ THEATERS

Theaters, including ㉙ the Globe and ㉚ the Swan, were built south of the river. The fire that burned down the Globe in 1613 began when a spark from a stage cannon landed on the thatched roof.

㉛ BEAR GARDEN

Bears, bulls, and even lions were cruelly forced to fight dogs here for entertainment and gambling.

NEW YORK CITY

The city of New York, with its gleaming skyscrapers and its grid of busy streets, has been a model for modern cities around the world.

NEW YORK CITY

Country: United States
Continent: North America
Estimated population:
8.3 million (New York City, 2018)
Founded in: 1626
Historic names: New Amsterdam, Manna-hata

WHO HAS LIVED THERE?

Maya Angelou (1928–2014) was born in St. Louis and was a performer, editor, civil rights activist, novelist, and poet. New York was one of many cities where she lived, and she owned a house in Harlem. Her work includes the famous memoir *I Know Why the Caged Bird Sings* and the poems "Awaking in New York" and "Harlem Hopscotch."

Arturo Alfonso Schomburg (1874–1938) was born in Puerto Rico and came to New York City in 1891. He championed black history, arts, and music. A prolific collector of documents, art, and artifacts relating to black history, he was also a key intellectual figure in the "Harlem Renaissance"—a black artistic and social movement.

Susan B. Anthony (1820–1906) was born in Massachusetts and campaigned tirelessly for women's suffrage in New York City. She appeared before every Congress between 1869 and 1906 to ask for an amendment to allow women to vote. This finally happened in 1920 when the 19th Amendment was passed.

NEW YORK CITY TODAY

The heart of **New York** is a long, narrow island called **Manhattan**. Its high-rise steel and glass towers overlook the **Hudson** and the **East Rivers**. The island is linked by bridges, subways, and ferries to the sprawling outer boroughs of **Brooklyn**, **Queens**, the **Bronx**, and **Staten Island**.

Even people who have never been to **Manhattan** have heard of its most famous streets and districts. The financial center of **Wall Street**, the theater district around **Broadway**, and the luxury shops of **Fifth Avenue** are often seen in films.

Central Park is a green haven from the busy streets, with lakes, fountains, and tree-lined paths.

New York City has many of the world's finest museums and galleries, and some amazing modern architecture. Its baseball teams are the **Mets** and the **Yankees**, and many New Yorkers follow the football teams the **Giants** and the **Jets**, who play eight miles away in New Jersey. New York's nickname? The **Big Apple**!

NEW YORK CITY 1931

New York City has always been a city of business and trade, but it has had its ups and downs. In the 1920s, when corporations were making big money, they planned to build high skyscrapers and luxury hotels.

A few blocks away from the most fashionable streets were factories, street markets, and run-down tenement housing.

In 1929 the stock market crashed. This triggered the **Great Depression**, an economic disaster in which people all over the world went hungry. By 1932, one in three **New Yorkers** was unemployed and many lived in makeshift settlements known as "Hoovervilles."

In New York, construction offered jobs to those who were desperate for wages.

Through good times and bad, **New Yorkers** have always known how to enjoy themselves. In what was known as the **Great Migration**, many **African Americans** left the South of the United States for northern cities during and after the First World War, and they brought a new sound called **jazz** to the clubs of **Harlem**.

The **Empire State Building**, at that time the world's tallest skyscraper, opened on May 1, 1931. A 1933 movie, *King Kong*, showed a giant ape climbing to the top!

NEW YORK CITY 1886

The United States' most famous landmark, the **Statue of Liberty**, overlooks **New York Harbor**. It was opened in October 1886. For many immigrants, the torch of freedom she holds would be their first glimpse of the **New World**.

Over 1.2 million people lived in **New York** at this time. It was still a city of horse-drawn carriages, but railways had transformed it in the 1850s–1860s. The first iteration of **Grand Central Terminal** opened in 1871. **Brooklyn Bridge**, completed in 1883, was the highest structure in the city until the first skyscrapers in the 1890s.

Before the **Declaration of Independence** in 1776, **New York** had been a British colony, and before that, it was a Dutch one, called **New Amsterdam**. Dutch traders first built a fort at the southern end of **Manhattan Island** in 1625–1626. The first European to see **Manhattan** is said to be Italian explorer **Giovanni da Verrazzano** in 1524.

Before the Dutch removed the original inhabitants, the area was home to the **Lenape** people and part of **Lenapehoking**.

FIND THE RED FLAG TO BEGIN YOUR TOUR OF THIS CITY IN LAYERS.

NEW YORK CITY TODAY

Amid the towering skyscrapers
are layers of the city's past.

1 ELLIS ISLAND
Now a museum, Ellis Island processed more than 12 million immigrants from 1892 to 1954.

2 STATUE OF LIBERTY
Liberty Island's massive monument to freedom towers over Upper New York Bay. Steps inside the statue take you up to the crown.

3 BRIDGES
A plethora of bridges cross the East River.

4 BROOKLYN
Home to 2.7 million New Yorkers, Brooklyn is now a center for tech companies, art, and design.

5 WALL STREET
This name is often used to describe the financial power of New York City and of the United States as a whole. The New York Stock Exchange, with its frantic trading floor, is located at 11 Wall Street.

6 ONE HUNDRED BARCLAY
Originally the New York Telephone Building, this skyscraper now houses luxury apartments.

7 ONE WORLD TRADE CENTER
New York City's tallest skyscraper soars to 1,776 ft./541 m. It opened in 2014, replacing the Twin Towers of the former World Trade Center, which were destroyed in a terrorist attack in 2001.

8 CITY HALL
This historic building houses the mayor's office.

9 CHINATOWN
This is the oldest of NYC's Chinese communities. The 19th century saw large numbers of Chinese immigrants.

10 TENEMENT MUSEUM
Two 19th-century tenement buildings are preserved as a museum to the many immigrants who lived there during the buildings' history.

11 FLATIRON BUILDING
This 22-story building dates from 1902. It is shaped like the clothing irons used at the time.

12 WASHINGTON SQUARE
Here Broadway meets Fourth Avenue, with a famous statue of George Washington.

13 WHITE HORSE TAVERN
This bar became popular with many writers in the 1950s, including Dylan Thomas and Jack Kerouac.

14 HIGH LINE
Once a raised freight railway, the old tracks have been converted into an elevated park.

15 MEATPACKING DISTRICT
Some traditional meatpacking businesses remain in

NEW YORK CITY TODAY

The heart of New York is a long, narrow island called Manhattan. Its high-rise steel and glass towers overlook the Hudson and the East Rivers. The island is linked by bridges, subways, and ferries to the sprawling outer boroughs of Brooklyn, Queens, the Bronx, and Staten Island.

Even people who have never been to Manhattan have heard of its most famous streets and districts. The financial center of Wall Street, the theater district around Broadway, and the luxury shops of Fifth Avenue are often seen in films.

Central Park is a green haven from the busy streets, with lakes, fountains, and tree-lined paths.

New York City has many of the world's finest museums and galleries, and some amazing modern architecture. Its baseball teams are the Mets and the Yankees, and many New Yorkers follow the football teams the Giants and the Jets, who play eight miles away in New Jersey. New York's nickname? The Big Apple!

NEW YORK CITY 1931

New York City has always been a city of business and trade, but it has had its ups and downs. In the 1920s, when corporations were making big money, they planned to build high skyscrapers and luxury hotels.

A few blocks away from the most fashionable streets were factories, street markets, and run-down tenement housing.

In 1929 the stock market crashed. This triggered the Great Depression, an economic disaster in which people all over the world went hungry. By 1932, one in three New Yorkers was unemployed and many lived in makeshift settlements known as "Hoovervilles."

In New York, construction offered jobs to those who were desperate for wages.

Through good times and bad, New Yorkers have always known how to enjoy themselves. In what was known as the Great Migration, many African Americans left the South of the United States for northern cities during and after the First World War, and they brought a new sound called jazz to the clubs of Harlem.

The Empire State Building, at that time the world's tallest skyscraper, opened on May 1, 1931. A 1933 movie, *King Kong*, showed a giant ape climbing to the top!

NEW YORK CITY 1886

The United States' most famous landmark, the Statue of Liberty, overlooks New York Harbor. It was opened in October 1886. For many immigrants, the torch of freedom she holds would be their first glimpse of the New World.

Over 1.2 million people lived in New York at this time. It was still a city of horse-drawn carriages, but railways had transformed it in the 1850s–1860s. The first iteration of Grand Central Terminal opened in 1871. Brooklyn Bridge, completed in 1883, was the highest structure in the city until the first skyscrapers in the 1890s.

Before the Declaration of Independence in 1776, New York had been a British colony, and before that, it was a Dutch one, called New Amsterdam. Dutch traders first built a fort at the southern end of Manhattan Island in 1625–1626. The first European to see Manhattan is said to be Italian explorer Giovanni da Verrazzano in 1524.

Before the Dutch removed the original inhabitants, the area was home to the Lenape people and part of Lenapehoking.

NEW YORK CITY TODAY

Amid the towering skyscrapers are layers of the city's past.

1 ELLIS ISLAND
Now a museum, Ellis Island processed more than 12 million immigrants from 1892 to 1954.

2 STATUE OF LIBERTY
Liberty Island's massive monument to freedom towers over Upper New York Bay. Steps inside the statue take you up to the crown.

3 BRIDGES
A plethora of bridges cross the East River.

4 BROOKLYN
Home to 2.7 million New Yorkers, Brooklyn is now a center for tech companies, art, and design.

5 WALL STREET
This name is often used to describe the financial power of New York City and of the United States as a whole. The New York Stock Exchange, with its frantic trading floor, is located at 11 Wall Street.

6 ONE HUNDRED BARCLAY
Originally the New York Telephone Building, this skyscraper now houses luxury apartments.

7 ONE WORLD TRADE CENTER
New York City's tallest skyscraper soars to 1,776 ft./ 541 m. It opened in 2014, replacing the Twin Towers of the former World Trade Center, which were destroyed in a terrorist attack in 2001.

8 CITY HALL
This historic building houses the mayor's office.

9 CHINATOWN
This is the oldest of NYC's Chinese communities. The 19th century saw large numbers of Chinese immigrants.

10 TENEMENT MUSEUM
Two 19th-century tenement buildings are preserved as a museum to the many immigrants who lived there during the buildings' history.

11 FLATIRON BUILDING
This 22-story building dates from 1902. It is shaped like the clothing irons used at the time.

12 WASHINGTON SQUARE
Here Broadway meets Fourth Avenue, with a famous statue of George Washington.

13 WHITE HORSE TAVERN
This bar became popular with many writers in the 1950s, including Dylan Thomas and Jack Kerouac.

14 HIGH LINE
Once a raised freight railway, the old tracks have been converted into an elevated park.

15 MEATPACKING DISTRICT
Some traditional meatpacking businesses remain in

what is now also an area of art and design.

16 MACY'S
Welcome to the biggest department store (by sales) in the United States!

17 UNION SQUARE
Open-air chess players are often found in this park in Greenwich Village.

18 CHRYSLER BUILDING
This 1930 skyscraper rises 1,046 ft./318 m.

19 EMPIRE STATE BUILDING
At 1,250 ft./381 m, this was the world's tallest building from 1931 to 1973.

20 HEARST TOWER
The design of this 2006 skyscraper saves energy.

21 BROADWAY
This long avenue is famous for theater.

22 NEW YORK PUBLIC LIBRARY
This is the third largest library system in the U.S., with its impressive main branch on Bryant Park.

23 ROCKEFELLER CENTER
Set in Midtown Manhattan, this plaza and cluster of skyscrapers opened in 1933.

24 UNITED NATIONS
Since 1952 New York has been the global headquarters of the United Nations (U.N.). The U.N. was set up in 1945 after the Second World War.

25 TIMES SQUARE
Bright lights in the big city! New Yorkers gather in this busy square to ring in the New Year.

26 TIME WARNER CENTER
This twin skyscraper was built in 2003.

27 COLUMBUS CIRCLE
Traffic flows around fountains and a monument to the Italian navigator Christopher Columbus.

28 LINCOLN CENTER
This complex was built in the mid–20th century. It is home to the Metropolitan Opera, the NYC Ballet, the New York Philharmonic orchestra, and others.

29 AMERICAN MUSEUM OF NATURAL HISTORY
This 150-year-old museum is the best place in New York to meet a dinosaur!

30 CENTRAL PARK
The green heart of Manhattan has a 20-acre lake.

31 METROPOLITAN MUSEUM OF ART
The "Met" collection contains over 2 million works of art from over 5,000 years of history.

32 THE GUGGENHEIM
Opened in 1959, this building designed by Frank Lloyd Wright houses famous works of modern art.

33 HARLEM
This large, rapidly changing district in Upper Manhattan has traditionally been a center of African-American culture.

NEW YORK CITY 1931

A city of good times, bad times, daring new buildings, and jazz.

❶ ELLIS ISLAND
From 1892 to 1954, over 12 million new immigrants arrived at Ellis Island for processing. Many were fleeing poverty and persecution in their homelands.

❷❸❹❺ BRIDGES
Rail and motor traffic transformed New York City. New bridges now crossed the East River, north of the original ❷ Brooklyn Bridge. ❸ Manhattan Bridge (1909) and ❹ Williamsburg Bridge (1903) joined Brooklyn with Manhattan. ❺ Queensboro (59th Street) Bridge was an impressive crossing to Queens.

❻ BROOKLYN
This borough was an industrial area. It suffered in the Depression years when factories closed.

❼ BATTERY PARK
The southern tip of Manhattan includes a park. Castle Clinton once housed a popular aquarium.

❽ WALL STREET
The financial center of New York City became famous in 1929 when the stock market crashed, leading to the Great Depression.

❾ NEW YORK TELEPHONE BUILDING
This skyscraper was built on Wall Street and completed in 1927 in the fashionable art deco style.

❿ WOOLWORTH BUILDING
Completed in 1913, this building was the highest in the world at 791 ft./241 m. until 1930.

⓫ CHINATOWN
In the 1930s this area of Lower Manhattan was already the home of many Chinese immigrants.

⓬ TENEMENTS
Before New York City began to build public housing in 1936, many people lived in overcrowded, run-down tenement buildings.

⓭ FLATIRON BUILDING
By the 1930s this was one of many high-rises.

⓮ THE TOMBS
Manhattan's prison was known as the Tombs.

⓯ UNION SQUARE
This square has a history of being used for rallies and public meetings.

⓰ SINGER BUILDING
Opened in 1908 as headquarters for the Singer sewing machine company, this skyscraper stood until 1967.

⓱ MACY'S
This huge department store sponsored its first Thanksgiving Day Parade in 1924. A giant balloon of

14 WHITE HORSE TAVERN
The second oldest continuously run bar in New York was built in 1880.

15 MARKETS
Large and noisy markets in this area included Washington Market and Gansevoort Market.

16 MEATPACKING DISTRICT
In 1869 ground-level steam trains were built to transport food to Lower Manhattan from this area of markets.

17 MACY'S
New York City's best-known department store began as a small grocery store in 1858. By 1877 it occupied the ground floors of 11 buildings.

18 THE "OLD MET"
The first home of the Metropolitan Opera was at 1411 Broadway. It opened in 1883.

19 GRAND CENTRAL DEPOT
The first big railway terminal here opened in 1871.

20 ST. PATRICK'S CATHEDRAL
Manhattan's landmark Roman Catholic cathedral was built in 1858–1879.

21 COLUMBIA UNIVERSITY
Founded as King's College in 1754, Columbia moved to 49th Street and Madison Avenue in 1857.

22 CENTRAL PARK
People liked ice-skating here in winter! The park was set up in 1857 and reached its present size in 1873.

23 AMERICAN MUSEUM OF NATURAL HISTORY
The first building in its current location opened in 1877. The museum organized many famous expeditions.

24 METROPOLITAN MUSEUM OF ART
From small beginnings in 1870, the "Met" grew into one of the world's greatest art museums. In 1886 the galleries in Central Park were only six years old.

25 NAVARRO FLATS
A world away from tenements, these apartments were the ultimate in 1880s luxury. The largest were around 7,000 sq. ft./650 sq. m., and they contained two bathrooms—rare at this time.

26 GRACIE MANSION
This fine house overlooking the East River was built as the country home of Archibald Gracie, a Scottish merchant, in 1799.

27 HARLEM
This Uptown district developed quickly thanks to elevated train lines ("els"), and many new houses were built here in the 1880s.

28 POLO GROUNDS
Used for baseball since 1883, the Polo Grounds was home to the Gothams. Renamed the Giants, they are still popular. Their home stadium is now in San Francisco.

FUTURE CITIES

What will cities look like in the future? The 1960s TV cartoon *The Jetsons* predicted that families would have flying cars, that robots would do housework, and that people would live in a city in the sky.

Most of us don't live in skyscrapers, and cars don't fill city skies, so what do we know about what cities might be like in the future? In the past cities were shaped by how they overcame challenges: the walls of Istanbul protected it from invasion and the skyscrapers of New York created more space in a place where land was scarce. Part of understanding how cities will evolve is understanding the challenges they face.

One major challenge for cities today is population growth. It is estimated that by 2050, 68 percent of humans will be living in urban areas. Larger numbers of people require more resources such as water, housing, and energy. Houses may get smaller, and many architects today are working on innovative designs for small living spaces. Another major challenge is air pollution caused by the burning of fossil fuels such as coal and oil. This is leading to potentially catastrophic climate change.

Future cities are going to have to be bigger and greener to face these issues. Many are already working on solutions. In some cities, more trees and "green walls" have been planted to filter out polluting carbon dioxide. The largest green wall in the world is

a 51,000-square-foot/5,300-square-meter wall at a college in Singapore, which helps to keep the building cool in the tropical heat. Other cities have excluded traffic from their centers. The use of renewable energy such as solar, wind, and tidal power is increasing around the world, and improved electric cars and buses are becoming more common.

The scarcity of resources caused by growing populations and climate change has also led to innovative solutions. In many places, including Dubai in the United Arab Emirates, seawater is made suitable for drinking. Urban farms and garden schemes have also become popular, such as the city farming scheme in Mumbai, India, which turns unused city spaces into urban farms.

Technology will affect the lives of future city dwellers in many ways. The greatest changes in future city life may involve electronic connectivity, artificial intelligence, and robotics. Inventions such as self-driving cars will transform both transport and employment. We may also be able to travel between cities much more quickly. The Hyperloop is a vacuum tunnel train, currently under development, which could be able to travel at 600 miles per hour. Like "maglev" trains, it will use magnets so it "levitates" and does not create friction on the track.

The cities of the future we see portrayed in science-fiction films or games are often places where everything has gone horribly wrong. It is up to us and future generations to make sure that we get things right.

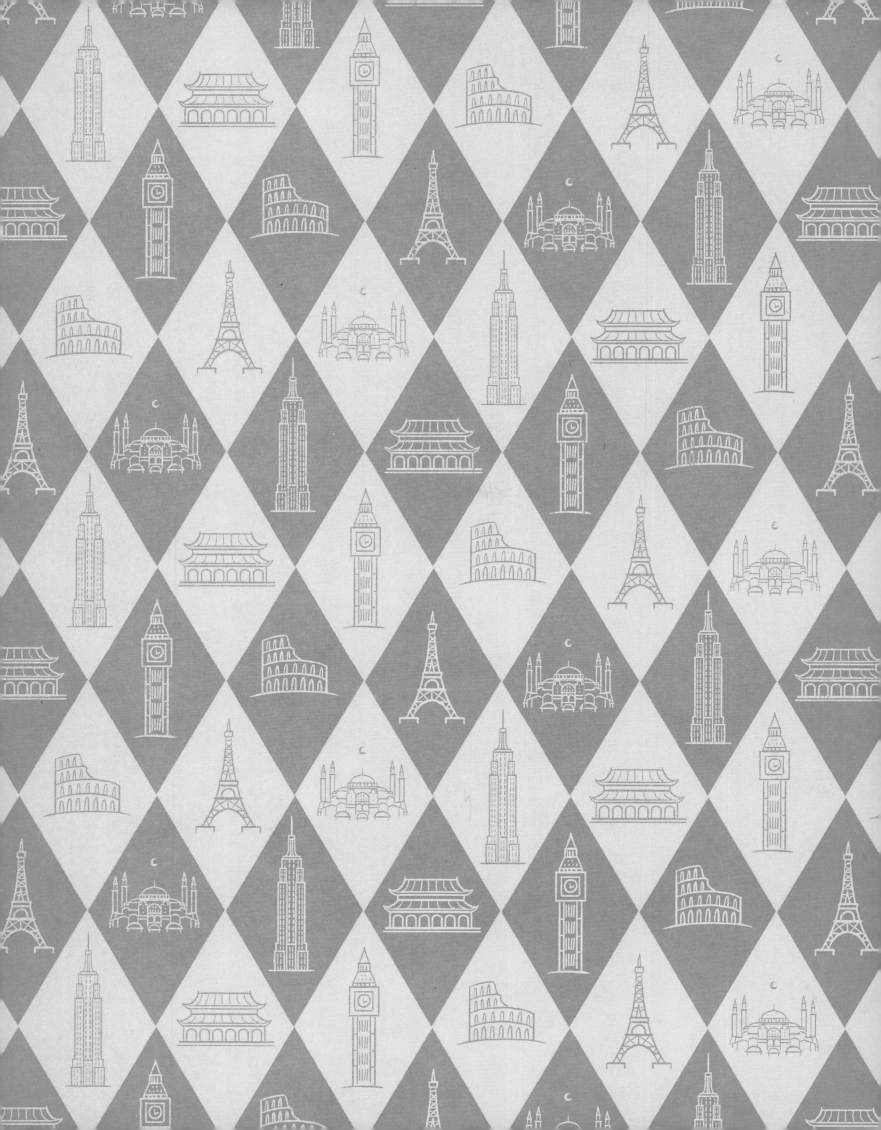